Presented to:

_____

From:

_____

Date:

_____

GodSpeaks™

Stories for Teens

Honor Books
Tulsa, Oklahoma

2nd Printing

GodSpeaks℠ *Stories for Teens*
ISBN 1-56292-846-5
Copyright © 2001 by Honor Books
P.O. Box 55388
Tulsa, Oklahoma 74155

Let's meet at my house Sunday before the game.
C'mon over and bring the kids.
What part of "Thou Shalt Not" didn't you understand?
We need to talk.
Keep using my name in vain, I'll make rush hour longer.
Loved the wedding, invite me to the marriage.
That "Love Thy Neighbor" thing . . . I meant that.
I love you. I love you. I love you.
Will the road you're on get you to my place?
Follow me.
Need directions?
You think it's hot here?
Tell the kids I love them.
Need a marriage counselor? I'm available.
Have you read my #1 best-seller? (There will be a test.)
Do you have any idea where you're going?
"Big Bang Theory"? You've got to be kidding.
My way is the highway.

REFERENCES

Contributing Writers

Honor Books would like to thank the following writers who contributed their stories to this book:

Teresa Cleary
Betty Steele Everett
Sherri Kukla
Nancy Rue
Kathryn Springer
Marlys G. Stapelbroek
Micah E. Stevens

Introduction

God has a lot to say, and He has said it pretty plainly within the framework of the Bible. But, despite the fact that the Bible is one of the best known and most widely read books on the planet, many people aren't familiar with how its concepts and principles apply to their everyday lives. This can be especially true for today's teenagers, who face a daunting and complex world of problems and possibilities.

If you are a teenager struggling to better understand God and how He can provide insight and wisdom for the choices you face each day, this book of stories has been designed for you. The statements attributed to God are, of course, not His actual words. They are statements that illustrate principles He teaches in the Bible. We hope they will cause you to meditate on God's character, question some of your preconceived notions, and discover for yourself the personal nature of His love for you.

If you have questions or would like to make comments, please feel free to contact us at our Web site: *www.GodSpeaks.org*

Table of Contents

Relax. I'm in control.
—GOD

A Matter of Teamwork

I didn't think much about it when the rain first started. Sure the weatherman had predicted severe thunderstorms and the possibility of flooding, but that was for people who lived close to the river. I thought we were too far away to be bothered. But the rain didn't stop, and some roads in our area had to be closed.

"This is pretty serious, isn't it?" my little sister, Kelly, asked my dad at breakfast.

"Duh," I answered.

Kelly stuck out her tongue at me, and Mom shot me "the look." She doesn't like it when I say that. In fact, there were a lot of things my parents didn't like lately. My attitude was one thing. My friends were another. My parents said they couldn't understand why I hung out with such a lowly group of guys when I had "nice" friends at church.

"If your friends aren't Christians, they're not going to act like Christians," my mom told me time and again.

She was right about that. The fun my friends liked to have was definitely not of the Christian variety. I'd been a believer long enough to know that. But instead of doing something about it, I just followed along—even though I couldn't say I felt good about what we had been doing and sometimes wondered if my parents weren't right after all.

My dad got up from the table. "We don't have anything to worry about," he assured Kelly as he left for work. "We're high and dry."

It was amazing how a couple of hours could change all that. The river rose faster than anyone had ever seen, and suddenly our part of town was being threatened.

Dad was back home at noon. "They're going to build a flood wall on the east side of town," he told Mom. "The river is really swelling. If we don't do something now, this whole town is going to be under water."

"Can I help?" I asked.

Dad and Mom exchanged looks. I was supposed to be grounded for being out with my friends past curfew the Friday before. I could see the two of them silently debating whether or not they should lift my restriction. "Sure," Dad finally said. "Get into your oldest clothes."

When I went to change, Dad told Mom to start packing. "We'd better be ready for anything."

The rain had turned to drizzle by the time Dad and I arrived at the flood-wall site.

"Look at all the people," I said. Some were shoveling sand into bags while others passed the bags to where the wall was being built.

"If we're going to turn this disaster around, it's going to take teamwork," Dad said. I nodded. "Take a place in line," Dad told me as he picked up a shovel. "I'm going to help fill bags."

The work was back breaking. The lady next to me would toss me a bag, and then I'd toss it to the guy next to me. There's nothing like passing sandbags to give you some perspective on life. I thought about the flood and what a disaster it would be if the water reached our house. I thought, too, about the disaster my life had become.

"Bet you could think of some things you'd rather be doing today," the guy next to me said.

Yeah," I agreed, "about a hundred."

He laughed. "I couldn't agree more." Then he stuck out his hand. "I'm Bill."

We shook hands. "Kyle."

"So, Kyle, why'd you decide to help?" the guy asked.

"Well, it was this or stay grounded," I told him. "I broke curfew last week."

"Not a good move," Bill added with the hint of a smile.

"You're telling me," I said, shaking my head. "You know, I can't remember the last time I made a good move. At least according to my parents. Why are you here?" I asked.

"Nowhere else to go," he said. "My house is under water."

"And you're here?" I was amazed.

"Seemed like the Christian thing to do."

"I guess it is," I said, surprised by his answer.

"The way I figure it," Bill continued, "I could be mad at God for letting all this happen, or I could ask Him to help me through it. Either way, my circumstances won't change. God's in charge, and I'm not. The only thing that I can change is my attitude."

I was quiet as I thought about what Bill had said. *Who's in charge of my life?* I wondered.

I almost laughed. That wasn't such a tough question. The church part was in God's hands, the friends part was in mine, and the punishment part—that was firmly in my parents' grasp. Meanwhile my life seemed to go from one disaster to another.

What was it my dad had said earlier? "If we're going to turn this disaster around, it's going to take teamwork." I knew he was right. But just as fighting a raging river was too big of a job for any one person to tackle alone, so was turning my life around. I needed help.

Lord, I can't do this job by myself, I prayed right there in the midst of the people and sandbags and raindrops. *I need Your help.*

I wish I could tell you that at the moment of my prayer, the sun broke through the clouds and a glorious rainbow appeared as a sign that God had heard me. But that didn't happen. There were still sandbags to pass and a river to fight. And someone said more rain was predicted for that night. But I knew it would be okay. None of us had to fight off disaster alone. It would be a team effort.

> *Do not be anxious about anything, but in everything, by prayer and petition, with thanksgiving, present your requests to God.*
>
> Philippians 4:6

God Speaks:

You can face any circumstance when you put your trust in Me.

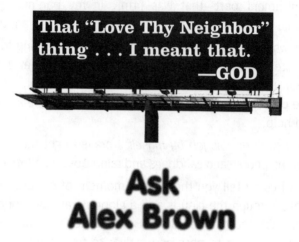

That "Love Thy Neighbor" thing . . . I meant that.
—GOD

Ask Alex Brown

"Hey, Becker, I must have missed the sale at the thrift shop over the weekend!"

Candace averted her eyes and scooted past Jill Masters and her friends. Their laughter followed her as she slipped into the room at the end of the hall. Justin Thomas, editor of the Lincoln *Leader,* was already talking to the group of students in the staff office.

"It's time for some changes, people. The *Leader* isn't just going to have a face-lift. We're talking major reconstructive surgery here. No more tired editorials and 'Student of the Month' stuff. We're going to give the kids at Lincoln High what they want." His voice rose dramatically. "We're going to give them real news. Relationships and exposés. You know what I'm talking about."

Candace was afraid she did.

"I'll be giving some of you individual assignments, but for now, start asking yourself—will this story cause people to stand in line for a copy of the *Leader?* If the answer is no, then write something else. We'll meet again tomorrow."

When she left the staff meeting, Candace deliberately went the long way to get to the library. *Coward,* she thought to herself. *You just don't want to run into one of Jill Master's insults.*

For some reason, Jill had taken an immediate dislike to Candace. She seemed to take personal delight in critiquing the way Candace dressed, the way she wore her hair—even the way she breathed.

It wouldn't have been so bad if Candace only had to deal with Jill at school. But, two weeks earlier, Candace and her family had moved in right next door to Jill.

That evening the phone rang, and Candace's mother beckoned to her.

"Hello?"

"Hey, Candy, this is Justin Thomas."

"Oh. Hi, Justin." *Candy?* she thought.

"I noticed you at the meeting this afternoon. I have an idea. What if we started an advice column in the paper? Everybody would eat it up. It would add a lot, don't you think? Here's the thing: I want you to do it."

"Me!" Candace squeaked. "You don't even know me. And I don't know many people at school yet," she protested.

"That's the beauty of it," Justin interrupted. "You're new at school. No preconceived ideas. We wouldn't use your real name, and no one would know it was you except Mrs. Wright and me."

"Justin—"

"I even thought of a column name. We could call it, "Ask Alex Brown." What do you think? Alex could be male or female, and Brown is a common name. There isn't an Alex Brown at school, either." Justin took a breath.

"Can I think about it?" Candace asked faintly.

"Sure. Bye, Alex Brown." Justin hung up.

"Friend of yours?" Candace's mom asked casually.

"That was Justin Thomas, editor of the school paper and human bulldozer," she explained grimly. "He wants me to write an advice column for the newspaper." Candace shook her head.

"I think you might be good at that sort of thing," her mom said slowly.

"You're kidding, right?" Candace asked in astonishment. "I mean, Mom, come on, I can't even solve my own problems!"

Mrs. Becker looked concerned. "What problems? Aren't you adjusting to your new school? Making friends?"

Candace laughed weakly. "I'm fine, Mom. Just the usual stuff, that's all."

The following week, Justin handed Candace a plastic bin full of envelopes.

Candace's eyes widened. "All these?"

"We can publish three letters per issue," Justin said. "Pick out the funny ones. Nothing too heavy or serious."

Candace was on her way home that afternoon when she saw Jill.

"Hey, it's early for trick-or-treating!" Jill sang out.

Candace looked down at her brown velvet dress and sighed. She loved vintage clothes. Obviously, that was what had singled her out from Jill and her friends.

When Candace arrived home, she sat down at the table and started to read some of the letters. Most of them were humorous. It was obvious from the "problems" that kids weren't taking "Alex Brown" very seriously. Candace began to relax. If that's the kind of help students wanted, then Justin's direction wasn't too far off.

"Oh, no!" Candace said as she read one letter again.

Dear Alex Brown,

Do you believe in God? I think he's mad at me because he's letting my parents split up. I don't know what to do. What do you think?

Wondering

Candace knew she couldn't answer this one. Justin would take her off the assignment if she did. She moved it to the bottom of the pile and tried to concentrate on a letter from "Desperately Wanting to Go to the Prom."

The following week, everyone was talking about Alex Brown. Who was he? Or she? Some people thought the columnist was Justin. The buzz was continuous. Letters began to pour into the *Leader's* office.

"You're really great at this, Candy," Justin said one afternoon.

"It's Candace," she corrected half-heartedly. "I think I should answer some of the serious ones, too, Justin."

"No one wants to read the serious stuff, Candy."

The next week, Candace was sitting at the kitchen table, sifting through a mountain of letters to Alex Brown, when her mother came in. Behind her was Jill Master's mother.

"Mrs. Masters and I are going out for a cup of coffee," Mrs. Becker said calmly.

"Okay." Candace said. She glanced at Mrs. Masters and looked away. It was obvious that Jill's mother had been crying.

Candace went back to her letters and came across the letter from "Wondering" again.

Someone wanted to know if Alex believed in God. Someone thought maybe God was mad at him or her. Someone needed to know that "yes, she does" and "no, He's not." Candace made a decision.

"Justin, I'm going to answer this letter." Candace held out the piece of paper to Justin the next day.

He read it and laughed. "You can have a lot of fun with this one. Go ahead."

"I'm not going to have fun with it," Candace said firmly.

That evening, Candace's mom mentioned that she was going out with Jill's mom again. "Candace, I'd like you to pray for the Masters. A few weeks ago, Mr. Masters left his family, and he wants a divorce from Jill's mom."

Candace looked down at the letter in front of her—the letter from "Wondering."

It couldn't be.

She picked up the letter and held it in her hand. "Mom, I've decided to answer this in person."

Mrs. Becker smiled. "I'll be praying."

Candace looked at the words again, remembered all the things Jill had said to her over the past month, and took a deep breath.

"Lord, You're going to have to help me with this one," she whispered.

Ten minutes later, Candace and Jill were face-to-face.

"What do you want?" Jill asked, but her voice was quiet, not hostile.

Candace held out the letter. "I came to answer this."

Jill stared at the letter and then at Candace. She looked upset. *"You're* Alex Brown?"

"Only if you're 'Wondering.'"

Jill didn't say anything for a few moments, and then she stepped back.

"Come on in." She smiled tentatively.

Candace smiled back, knowing God would take care of the rest.

"Love your enemies and pray for those who persecute you."

Matthew 5:44

God Speaks:

I am pleased when you show love to those who have treated you badly.

Back to the Future

Marc sat on the sofa, staring past the flickering TV screen.

How could Heather just suddenly say we should break up? he asked himself for the thousandth time. *After all we've meant to each other for six months! I thought we really had something. Now she decides we shouldn't be together for a while. And she says she can't tell me why because she doesn't know herself!*

Marc turned away from the TV. A guy in high school doesn't cry—not even if his whole world has blown up in his face.

He tried to act normally at dinner, but the little he ate tasted like cardboard.

"You sick or somethin'?" his younger brother, Jason, asked.

"No!" Marc snapped. "Just leave me alone!"

His father gave him a look that said he'd better knock it off right then, and even his grandmother looked at him with surprise. Marc didn't care. They wouldn't understand how he felt even if he told them. They couldn't know how much he cared about Heather. Just being with her at youth group or walking together between classes was worth waiting all day for.

In his room later, Marc pulled books from his backpack, but he couldn't concentrate. All he could think of was when he had taken Heather home that afternoon. She had been so quiet. He knew right away that something was wrong, but he had been sure he could fix whatever it was. Then she stunned him by saying she didn't want to see him anymore.

"There's no one else, Marc. It's just . . . well, I think we should cool it for a while and date other people."

For a second, Marc had been speechless. Then his hurt became anger. "Fine with me! See you around!" He had stormed out, swallowing to keep back the tears.

Now Marc took a deep breath and reread the first paragraph of the history assignment. It still made no sense.

A sudden knock at the door made him jump. Maybe Heather had called to say it was all a stupid mistake and she couldn't live without him any more than he could without her.

But it was his grandmother's soft voice that answered his "Who is it?" Marc fought back disappointment. "Come on in."

His grandmother had moved in with Marc's family a month before, and it was working out well for everyone.

"Do you need anything, Gram?" He didn't want to talk to anyone right then.

"I thought maybe you might, Marc."

"What would I need?" Marc asked sharply.

"I watched you at dinner. Something's wrong, and since you got home so early today, I thought it might be about you and Heather."

"How did you know?" Marc stared at his grandmother.

She smiled. "I guess I just felt it." She took his hand in her smaller, blue-veined one. "Do you want to talk about it?"

"There's nothing you can do, Gram."

"I can pray about whatever it is. God knows your problem even if I don't."

"Heather dumped me. And I thought we were perfect together."

"That is hard," his grandmother agreed. "You probably feel angry at her and the whole world right now."

"I sure do! But how did you know that?"

"Marc, come to my room in a few minutes. I have something to show you."

For the next few minutes, Marc tried to read his assignment while wondering what his grandmother had to show him. She hadn't brought much with her when she moved in.

When he had given his grandmother twelve minutes, Marc went down the hall to her room.

"Here it is," his grandmother said, holding out an old envelope. "It's a letter your dad wrote me from church camp the summer he was a counselor."

"A letter from Dad?" Marc pulled out the single sheet.

Dear Mom,

I've met a great girl here! Her name's Shelley, and she's a great Christian. She loves water sports and music and everything else I like. She's beautiful too.

Marc stopped. "'Mom? I knew they met at a church camp, but why show me this now?"

"Read on and you'll see."

You know, I didn't plan to come here. Before Jan broke up with me, I wanted to stay home so I could be with her all summer. Then, when she said it was over, I took this job just to get away. I guess I wasn't much fun to be with, Mom. And I didn't believe it when you said God had something better for me. Now I know you were right! I'm free to be with Shelley, and she's a lot more fun! I'll bring her home our first day off, so you and Dad can meet her. You'll love her!

Marc stared at the letter. "A girl dumped Dad? But he was better looking than I am. He played football and was even class president. He had everything going for him. Why would anyone dump him?"

"Maybe so he could meet your mother," his grandmother said quietly.

"Yeah." Marc could not imagine anyone but his mother married to his father.

"Of course, this happened months later," his grandmother pointed out. "It didn't happen right away, and he was miserable for a while. Marc, I know it sounds too simple, but God really does work things out for our good. We don't usually see it right away because we're shortsighted. We only see what's happening now. God sees our whole future. Of course, it's still going to be hard for you when you see Heather, especially if she's with someone else."

"It will." Marc was dejected again.

"It may take a long time for you to see this as anything but a catastrophe, so in the meantime, why not get busy with things you've been wanting to do but didn't have time for because you were always with Heather? Like taking your guitar out of the closet or going cross-country skiing again. Heather never enjoyed that, but you have other friends who do. And I hear they need help with some odd jobs at the church."

Marc shook his head. None of that would make him forget Heather. Yet he had enjoyed skiing and playing the guitar. It couldn't hurt to try them again.

"Thanks." He kissed her cheek. "But why did you save that letter all these years?"

His grandmother smiled and, to Marc's surprise, winked at him. "The Lord must have known I'd need it again someday."

"My thoughts are not your thoughts, neither are your ways my ways," declares the LORD. *"As the heavens are higher than the earth, so are my ways higher than your ways and my thoughts than your thoughts."*

Isaiah 55:8-9

God Speaks:

I can see your today and your tomorrow. I am constantly working to bring about the very best for your life.

OK, break it up!

—GOD

Breaking Up
Fights Is Hard To Do

"There's a fight!"

"Where?"

"Locker hall."

I watched in disgust from the corner of A wing as two guys duked it out with a crowd smothering them on all sides. I rolled my eyes and walked past the outskirts of the jeering mob.

With a swish of raw silk, a figure rammed past me, high heels tapping the tile as she shoved through the throng. I stared as Dr. Cutter, our vice principal, flung kids aside, two at a time by the backs of their T-shirts. "Get back—all of you!" she yelled. "Break it up!"

I feel that way sometimes, I thought as I moved on toward the lunchroom. *All I do is break up fights.* From the cafeteria doorway, I craned my neck for Ming and Damien at the debaters' table. There they were—my two best friends—Damien pounding his index finger on the table like the district attorney and Ming sitting back with his arms folded across his chest like the counsel for the defense.

"You use that argument and you'll have both of us thrown out of the round—"

"And if you use yours, we'll be out of the tournament totally because they'll laugh us out!"

You'd have thought they were arch rivals—instead of debate partners—the way the veins were bulging in Damien's neck and the cheek muscles were twitching in Ming's face.

"Hi, guys," I said. "Trouble in paradise?"

"Yeah," Ming said. "Not enough cheese on these tacos." He stood up, greasy tortillas in hand.

Damien shook his head. "He sure gets his jockeys in a bunch before a tournament."

"You, of course, are the picture of serenity."

"Come on, Joanna. I make one suggestion, and he goes off like—"

"All I wanted was a spoonful of processed cheese, and I practically had to show the woman my driver's license," Ming said from behind us.

"I need salsa," Damien said, standing up abruptly and heading for the counter.

"Man, what's eating him?" Ming questioned.

"You guys are both stressed out," I said. I could hear my voice going into its soothe mode. "It's almost the end of the semester, and you've got this big tournament this weekend."

Ming watched Damien move back toward the table. "Okay, I'll try to be cool."

Damien and Ming had been friends since elementary school. We'd all gotten together in our freshman year when I'd joined the debate team. They competed for everything from girls to test scores. It seemed so stupid to me, but I always felt like I had to fix it.

At first I just steered the conversation onto neutral territory. When we ran out of that, I started taking each one of them aside and trying to enlighten him on how the other one was feeling. I discovered that when I went into my soothe mode, they'd back off of each other—for a while.

That night as I was going over my piece for the tournament in my room, the lines slipped out of my head, and an idea slid in. Maybe there was another approach—one that might last longer.

I went downstairs and asked my parents if I could have Ming and Damien over Thursday night.

"Practice?" Dad asked.

"More like a peace conference. Damien and Ming are into this one-upmanship thing. Everything's a contest, and it's driving me nuts. I thought I'd give them a present—to remind them that they're friends instead of opponents."

"Sure, go for it," Dad said. "But beware. Making peace can be a rough business."

Ming and Damien were already bickering when I let them in Thursday night—something about Ming's driving. But I knew as soon as they saw Mom's homemade enchiladas, they'd start melting.

"Hey, Joanna," Ming began, "are you aware that there's a tree in the middle of your coffee table?"

"No way!" I said.

"Let me get rid of it for you," Damien said. He snatched up the two-foot tree, and Ming grabbed for it, but Damien held it high over his head.

"Go ahead, wreck it," I said calmly. "It's your tree."

"Ours?" Damien asked. They examined it with debaters' eyes.

"Hey—cool! It's all—us!"

"Where'd you get these miniature trophies?"

"Man, are these actual movie tickets from stuff we saw?"

"Wait—tell me these aren't made out of straws from Papa John's."

"Hey, Jo," Ming said. "Thanks for putting these little soccer balls on here for me. I'd almost forgotten I ever played soccer."

Damien jabbed him. "You obviously forgot I ever played soccer. They're on there for both of us."

"We all try to forget you played soccer, Damien. You stunk."

"Oh." Damien plucked off one of the tiny plastic baseball caps. "Then shall we go on to discuss your stellar baseball career?"

"Stop it!" I shouted.

They looked up from the tree with stunned faces. Neither of them had ever heard me yell before.

"Just stop it! I try to do something to show you two what you mean to each other, and you even turn that into one of your stupid arguments. I'm sick of it!" I hurled my last sentence over my shoulder as I stormed out. "If you want a friendship anymore, you're going to have to fix it yourselves!"

I cried for half an hour, but it didn't make me feel any better. My only consolation was the fact that they were gone when I came back out. Only Dad was in the family room, studying my tree.

"It was a stupid idea," I said, flopping miserably into a chair. "And I blew it. I could've done something besides explode! I actually told them they needed to fix it themselves."

"God would have told them the same thing," Dad said. The Bible says that if there's a problem between two people, they have a responsibility to work it out. We are to live in peace."

I studied Dad's face. "Then you think I did the right thing, telling them to deal with it?"

"Things won't get better until they decide to make it better," he said.

The next morning when Mom came in to wake me up, she was carrying a pathetic-looking two-foot tree with a bunch of stuff on it.

"This was on the front porch this morning," Mom said. "The card says it's for you."

"Jo," the card read, "we stayed up all night and—well, it isn't pretty, but this is what we came up with. Thanks for showing us we're jerks. Damien and Ming"

Mom gave a snort. "Snowflakes cut from Papa John's napkins? Little boxing gloves?" She went on grunting over peace signs cut from aluminum cans and a magnet shaped like a taco. But I didn't hear most of it. I was studying the pint-sized certificate they'd done on Ming's computer.

"PEACE PRIZE AWARD TO JOANNA OLDFIELD FOR MAKING US GET OVER OURSELVES."

"You have interesting friends, Joanna," Mom said. "You weren't planning on putting this in the living room, were you?"

"No way!" I said. This was staying right here to remind me that keeping the peace can be a pretty tough business.

Make every effort to keep the unity of the Spirit through the bond of peace.

Ephesians 4:3

God Speaks:

Commit your heart to a life of peace with those around you.

Don't make me come down there.

—GOD

Burdens

"**M**om," I wailed, "get him out of here—now!"

I stood in the doorway of my room, fists clenched, eyes shut, yelling. I didn't used to yell much, but now my new ten-year-old foster brother drove me to it regularly.

Randy squirmed past me to get out of my bedroom as Mom rushed in to see what the commotion was all about. Randy almost knocked Mom over as he squeezed past her in the narrow hallway. The front door slammed hard, rattling the living-room windows.

In my room I leaned my head against the closet door. "I've had it!" I yelled.

"Susan." Mom breathed the word like a sigh.

"No! I'm tired of trying to be patient," I said before she could say anything else. "He doesn't understand the word 'no.' Why'd you have to bring him here? He's ruining my life!"

Mom stood quietly for so long I finally raised my head to see if she was still in the room. She stared out the window. When she turned to meet my gaze, her consoling smile couldn't hide the tired look in her eyes. "I don't know what to tell you," she admitted.

I felt a twinge of guilt.

"I'll go check on Randy," Mom said, closing my bedroom door behind her.

Sighing deeply, I plopped onto my bed. Outside the gloomy sky slowly gave way to darkness. Usually I loved the brisk fall days, but this year the whole house seemed to be constantly in an uproar—all because of one ten-year-old brat.

When my older brother left for college last year, Mom and Dad started talking about becoming foster parents. I had just turned fifteen, and I admit, I don't always listen when they talk to me. So every time this "foster" thing came up, I said, "Yeah, sure, sounds like it'll make you happy." Mostly, I just said enough to get out of the conversation.

It's not like I was totally ignorant though. I knew this meant having other kids around. But since I pretty much kept to myself, I thought that's what the foster kid would do too. I couldn't have been more wrong!

The slam of the front door interrupted my thoughts. Muffled voices moved down the hallway.

"I'm sorry, I won't do it again," Randy whined.

Yeah, right, I thought.

I skipped dinner that night so I wouldn't have to see Randy. The next morning I left before he woke up.

"I'm telling you, Kimberly," I moaned as we waited for the bus, "I'm sick of this foster-kid thing. He is driving me nuts."

We shivered in the cold morning air. I buttoned all the buttons on my coat.

"Nice coat," Kimberly said.

I groaned. "Kimmie, you aren't even listening!"

Little wisps of steam puffed from our mouths as we spoke.

"Did your mom buy that for you?" Kimberly asked.

"Yes, my mom bought me the coat," I practically yelled. "So what?"

Kimberly didn't seem bothered by my anger. I guess she's seen a lot of it lately.

"You don't even see my point, do you?" she asked.

"What is your point?"

"Randy hasn't had the kind of parents you've had," she said. "It's not his fault he behaves like he does."

"Don't lay a guilt trip on me, Kimmie," I pleaded. "I feel guilty enough. You just don't know what it's like."

"I've got a little brother, too, you know."

"That's different," I said.

"You're right," Kimmie said. "But the Bible says we're supposed to bear one another's burdens."

I was glad to see the bus pull up, so I didn't have to answer. I know Randy's life has been bad, but talk about burdens. That's the perfect word to describe him.

Later that day in English, Angela Barrett invited me to a party after the game that Friday. Normally I wouldn't even be invited to a party with football players and cheerleaders, but Angela and I had sort of become friends this year. At least we had talked to each other in English class.

"Are you sure you'll have fun there, Susan?" Kimberly, the spoilsport, asked me during lunch. "You won't even know anyone."

"I know Angela," I said.

"Yeah, sort of," Kimmie said. "But just knowing someone doesn't make her your friend."

The next day I could hardly wait to get to English to talk to Angela about the party. She was late getting to class, but as soon as she took her seat, I leaned over and whispered, "What are you wearing to the party?"

She looked at me kind of funny and shrugged.

"I think I'm going to go shopping and get something new," I whispered.

"Okay," she said.

I started to say something else but saw the teacher looking at me. Later, when he was helping a student in the front row, I resumed my conversation. "So, do you want to go shopping with me?".

She looked confused. "Shopping?"

"Yeah," I said, "for the party."

"It's just a little get-together after the game," she said, "it's no big deal."

She rolled her eyes and then looked interested in her English book.

Maybe she's just having a bad day, I thought. *Maybe that's why she was late to class.*

"Angela," I whispered. "Why were you late to class?"

"What are you, my mother?" she snapped.

The bell rang soon after that, and Angela took off. But when I got outside the door, I saw her standing there. "Hey, Susan," she said.

I realized then that she probably just didn't want to talk in class so she wouldn't get in trouble. Cheerleaders have to keep their grades up, or they can get kicked off the squad.

I smiled, "Yeah?" I said.

"I'm kinda rethinking that party invitation." She smiled sweetly.

"Yeah?"

"I don't think you should come after all," she said, still smiling. "I didn't know inviting you to a little party would turn you into such a pest." She held out her English and math books and said, "I've got enough burdens at school without inviting a burden to a party."

She quit smiling. "Get my point? Consider the party off limits." Then she turned and walked away.

My cheeks burned as I hurried off in the opposite direction, my eyes down. I couldn't bear to look to see if anyone heard.

"Susan," a familiar voice called out behind me. "Wait up!"

I slowed down just a little as Kimmie caught up.

She put her arm around my shoulders and walked along with me.

"You heard?" I finally squeaked out, trying to hold back tears.

"Yeah," she whispered.

"She called me a burden!" I whispered back.

Kimmie squeezed my shoulder, and we kept walking until we reached the end of the sidewalk and stood near the fence.

I wiped my eyes and then looked up at her.

"You know what?" I said. "I need to be kinder to Randy."

"Really?"

"Yeah," I said, feeling a little better. "I guess I know now what it feels like to be the oddball, to not belong."

"And how does that feel?"

"Not very good at all," I said.

Each of us will give an account of himself to God. Therefore let us stop passing judgment on one another. Instead,

make up your mind not to put any stumbling block or obsta-
cle in your brother's way.

Romans 14:12-13

God Speaks:

If you knew that tomorrow you would have to give an accounting to Me for your life, what would you change?

You look like you could use a faith-lift.
—GOD

A Change of Plans

"**H**ey, Julie, why don't you call me back when you've lost about a hundred pounds!" Russ said.

My face burned as I heard guys laughing in the background just before he slammed the phone down.

Russ and I had been friends since we were born. We had no choice. Our dads were best friends. Every time they visited, we visited.

But since my dad died, I hadn't seen Russ very often. And it was true that I was gaining weight. The counselors said it was a natural reaction to the stress. But that didn't make it any easier to deal with.

My dad got sick when I was in the seventh grade. My weight started coming on slowly. But through his two-year battle with cancer, and then in the year since he died, I had managed to put on enough weight that I was pretty uncomfortable with how I looked. And it was right at a time in my life when I was hoping to have a boyfriend. Who wants to start high school without any boyfriend prospects in sight? That's why I had called Russ. He wasn't exactly my idea of "perfect boyfriend" material, but when you're desperate—well, I guess you just lower your standards.

The next morning was Sunday, and though I really liked my youth group, I just couldn't work up the usual enthusiasm. After that phone call, all I did was mope and, I hate to admit it even to myself, eat.

If I couldn't have a boyfriend, at least I could have a Hershey bar. But as much as I like chocolate, even I could see a problem with that logic.

I remembered Pastor Mark, our youth pastor, said we should do what's right even when we don't feel like it. So I forced myself out of bed and got ready for church. "But I know I'll just have to look at all the couples in class," I grumbled to God while I was in the shower. It seemed like everybody was a "couple" except for me. It might have seemed like a funny thing to talk to God about, but I told God everything! In fact, He was the only One in the world who knew that my weight bothered me. I told everybody else I liked myself this way. And God also knew my deepest secret about how badly I wanted a boyfriend.

I wasn't ready for what I saw when I got to church. Out in the parking lot there were these pictures of kids. Posters of kids. Life-size cardboard cutouts of kids. They were in the hallway too. And on the walls in the stairwell. And more in the hall upstairs leading to the youth group. They all had messages on them—"God wants you! God needs you! God has a job for you!" And the last one was on a poster right next to the door into our classroom—"God has a mission in mind for you!"

"Did anyone notice anything unusual coming into church today?" Pastor Mark asked.

I laughed along with all of the rest of the kids in the class, and he didn't wait for our obvious answer.

"What do you have that the kids in these pictures don't have?" Pastor Mark said.

"Bad grades!" someone called out.

Then others joined in, "Braces!"

"Too much homework!"

"You're all right," Pastor Mark said, smiling. "Those kids don't have any of those things. They also don't have the opportunity to laugh." He walked over and picked up a couple of smaller photos, holding them up. "They don't have shoes—or even much food."

He set the pictures down, and sitting on the edge of his stool, he spoke very quietly.

"You know, some of you kids show up at church every Sunday because your parents make you come. But these kids don't even have parents."

The room was quiet except for some scuffling feet and a few coughs. Pastor Mark stared around the room, making eye contact with nearly every one of us. Suddenly, I wasn't even aware of the "couples" in the room.

"I bet every one of you in this room is dealing with some type of problem right now," Pastor Mark continued.

He smiled. "Isn't that right?" Heads started nodding. "And probably some of them are pretty big problems—problems you've asked God to help you with?"

I stared down at the floor because I was afraid he could read my mind. It seemed as if he already had.

"Well, today just may be the day God answers your prayer," Pastor Mark said.

By the time class was over that morning, I was one of seven kids who signed up to go on a "mission with God." Pastor Mark had explained that sometimes when we're dissatisfied with our lives, it's God telling us that He has something planned for us. And it usually isn't what we have planned. I had a funny feeling that if I was brave enough to explain my boy problem, Pastor Mark would say that was exactly what he was talking about.

All week long, I looked forward to the Saturday expedition to the orphanage in a small town just past the Mexican border. I don't think I even thought about guys or food that week. I was so excited about finding out what God had in store for me. And by the time we returned home that Saturday afternoon, I knew for sure that God had been speaking to me, just as our youth pastor had said.

"Pastor Mark," I said, "I want to work at the orphanage every Saturday. I just can't describe the feeling I had as soon as we got out of the van. When I saw those kids, looked at how they were living—well I couldn't think about anything except helping them. I know that's what God wants me to do."

"Julie, I gave that message last Sunday to fifty kids," Pastor Mark said. "Seven were willing to explore the possibility that God has a mission for them. But only two are willing to accept the mission. I'm thrilled to see you discover God's will for your life today."

He patted me on the shoulder and then handed me the clipboard to add my name to his very short list. The only other name on the clipboard was Jason, the only boy in the youth group who ever even talked to me.

Jason obviously has a heart for God. And who knows, I thought, with a smile, *maybe in time even a heart for me.*

Why are you downcast, O my soul? Why so disturbed within me? Put your hope in God, for I will yet praise him, my Savior and my God.

Psalm 42:11

God Speaks:

Even when it doesn't seem like it, I am always working in the midst of your circumstances.

Chicken Wings and Sex

"**W**innie!" Michael called out behind me.

"What?" I shouted—and felt my whole body being bowled over. I went head over heels three times and inhaled at least a half-gallon of salt water and sand. I think he must have said, "Watch out for that breaker."

I landed right at his feet in one crazy slide across the hard sand.

"Are you okay?" he asked.

"Yeah."

"Klutz. Can you get up?"

"Yeah."

"Want a hand?"

"Want a punch in the mouth?" We grinned at each other as I pulled myself up to a standing position. Blood was running down the side of my thigh, and the skin was practically yelping at the invasion of salt and sand into the wound.

"You better go back to the house and get that cleaned up. Want me to go up with you?"

"Nah." I shook my head. "You'd miss too much tanning time."

"Maybe Terri could go."

"I'd have to have a fractured skull before I could tear her away from Lee. Those two need to be surgically removed from each other." I grinned and headed up the beach.

No chance of you and I ever having to be surgically removed from each other, I thought as I started up the path toward the house. But I shrugged that off. I wasn't here to snag Michael Cannell into romance. The other thirteen people from my church youth group, plus our advisor, and I were here to have fellowship around the barbecue every night and improve our snorkeling and body surfing. I was just thankful Terri hadn't seen me take that dive. She'd still be laughing.

And then, as I entered the house, I thought I heard her laughing. I stopped on the bottom step and listened. There was no way. Terri was down on the waterfront somewhere. But I heard it again. It was Terri's giggle, coming from one of the boys' rooms on the first floor. Then I heard Lee's laugh. Terri and Lee were in his room together.

What should I do? Bust in on them like the vice squad? Pretend I didn't hear them and hightail it out of there, still oozing blood? I backed down the steps and listened again. Maybe I was wrong—but Terri giggled, and something smothered it. I lurched for the door and ran smack into the rack we used for our towels. The whole thing turned over on the tile floor with a heavy thud. I scrambled up the steps, and all I heard below was Terri whispering loudly, "Lee, there's somebody here!" I hid in the bathroom until my blood clotted. When I came out, they were gone.

Man, after all our talks about how we were both going to wait for marriage, and I'd practically caught her in the act. On a church trip, no less! The minute I turned out the light in our room that night, Terri wanted to know.

"It was you who knocked over the towel rack this afternoon, wasn't it?" she asked.

I came up on one elbow, and before I could censor myself, I blurted out, "Terri—are you still a virgin?"

There was only a split second of silence before she said indignantly, "Of course I am!"

She snapped on the light and sat facing me. "Look, Lee and I have—fooled around a lot—but we haven't actually, you know, done it—and we don't plan to. Technically speaking, I am still a virgin."

"Oh," I said, stupidly.

She sighed in a big-sisterly way. "You can't judge me, Winnie," she said. "When you feel about somebody like I do about Lee, you'll find out how hard it is to just hold hands."

This time I didn't even say "oh." She sighed again and turned out the light.

By the next day at lunchtime, I was more exhausted from seesawing back and forth in my mind than I was from mastering the boogie board. Where did Terri get off thinking she was so much wiser than I, just because she was "experienced"? Did she know something I didn't when it came to how far you should go with a boy? I spotted Michael sitting at a table in front of the food stands, and he smiled and waved me over. I did feel about somebody the way she did about Lee. But would I make the same decision she had?

"Is your surfing going that bad?" Michael asked when I sat down.

"Nah," I said. I unwrapped my corn dog without interest. He dove into his second plate of chicken wings.

"Man, I used to be satisfied with half an order of these," he said as he stuffed one in. "Now I need at least two before I can stop.

I stared at him. "Do you think that's the way people feel about sex?"

"Excuse me?" He acted surprised.

"You must need to do more and more until you're satisfied," I said.

"I wouldn't know, Winnie," he said. "Would you?"

"I'm talking about Terri, fool. When I went back to the house yesterday, they were in Lee's room. She told me last night that they haven't, you know—"

"Gotcha."

"But that it's okay because they do a lot of other stuff and she's still a virgin."

Michael stopped in mid-bite. "Do you think they're up there now?"

"Probably."

He put the wing on the plate and wiped the grease off his fingers. "I feel like we ought to do something."

"What? Go in there with a warrant?"

He frowned, and then his face lit up. He grabbed the plate of wings with one hand and my arm with the other. "No," he said. "We go in with a plate of wings."

When we came through the kitchen door, Terri was sitting at the counter, and startled, she jumped a foot in the air. She couldn't hide the fact that her next glance was a nervous one past us to the door.

"Looking for Lee?" Michael asked.

She glared at me. "Thanks, Winnie," she said. "He's supposed to meet me here."

"Terri, if this isn't wrong, how come you have to sneak around?" I quizzed.

"Chicken wings anyone?" Michael said quickly. He plucked one out of the pile and went to work on it. "Here's the deal," he said. "I can eat all of these I want because even once they're gone, I can always order more. But once something like, say, your virginity is gone, that's it—you can't get another one."

Terri gave me a dark look. "I told you that I'm still a virgin, and I'm planning to stay that way," her eyes narrowed. "I didn't expect you to share that information with the world."

"So the point is," Michael went on, "it won't be long before you either have to give up Lee or give up being a virgin. In that respect, it is like eating chicken wings."

"What are you talking about?" Terri's husky voice wound up angrily, but Michael plowed on.

"I can't sit here and look at these things and not eat them because I love them. Used to be I could be content with a few, but now—I gotta have the whole thing."

"So you're telling me that even though I'm not actually having sex with Lee, it's still wrong?" She rolled her eyes. "Well, since you two are such experienced lovers—"

"I don't have to be experienced to know it's wrong in God's eyes," I said. "Just like I don't have to steal or murder to know that if I do, I'm just going to end up hurting myself and somebody else in the end. That's what the commandments are for."

"The way I see it," Michael continued, "why tempt yourself?"

He was toying with a chicken wing, but he didn't seem interested in eating it anymore. I studied the countertop, and Terri sat with her arms folded across her chest.

"We ought to get back." Michael said finally.

I looked at Terri. "You coming with us?"

She didn't look back as she shook her head.

That was all either one of us said for most of the afternoon, except for that one moment on the beach blanket when Michael turned to me and said, "I don't want you to think I'm judging Lee.

I might do the same thing if I were in his place." He looked down at his hands. "That's why I don't get myself in the same situation."

I stifled a smile. That definitely explained a lot.

But I was still feeling like a piece of cardboard that night when I turned out the light before Terri came into the room. She'd been avoiding me all evening, and I wanted to be asleep before she started sighing at me.

I was still awake, though, when she came in and, to my surprise, sat on the edge of my bed.

"Thanks for caring," she said. "What you and Michael said really did make sense. I even tried to explain it to Lee. He didn't get it," she said. "We broke up."

"I'm sorry, Terri," I said. "I know you probably don't believe it, but I am."

"It's okay, really. I thought he was different—but he isn't, so— that's it, and I'm fine."

She wasn't. I could tell by the stiff sound in her voice. But I knew Terri—she didn't want sympathy. She'd handle it her own way.

"Hey," I said. "Did you eat those chicken wings?"

"No. They're in the fridge."

"Let's go for it," I said.

Marriage should be honored by all, and the marriage bed kept pure.

Hebrews 13:4

God Speaks:

There are some things in life that are worth waiting for. Sex is one of the best. Show it the respect it deserves.

> **You're always welcome.**
> **—GOD**

The Chilling Effect
of Prayer

Nikes thundered up the stairs behind me. "Jeffrey Gilmore," I shouted, "if you run in the house one more time—" I left the threat unfinished. Jeffrey had been unfazed by every punishment I could think of. Sighing, I admitted I should have been suspicious when his parents offered me nearly twice the going rate to baby-sit.

"Neh-neh, neh-neh, neh, neh. Cindy can't catch me." A hard yank on my hair told me just how close he was.

"Maybe she can!" I shouted, whirling around and grabbing for him. I actually had him for a moment, but Jeffrey was a nine-year-old eel. He slipped away, racing down the stairs and into the living room.

"No, she can't," he taunted.

Angry and frustrated, I scrambled after him. "Come here you—" The words froze in my mouth. Jeffrey was headed for the front door. It was warm for February, so I'd left it open, but I'd locked the glass storm door to feel a little safer.

"Jeffrey, don't—" I shrieked, watching in horror as he straight-armed the glass door, expecting it to pop open. Instead, his arm smashed through the glass.

"Yeowwww!" Jeffrey's cry energized me. I leaped forward, wrapping my arms around him. Sobbing, Jeffrey clung to me.

A dozen scratches oozed blood, but one long, deep cut above his elbow was gushing. What had I done? How had I let this happen?

Jeffrey's low moan cut through the fog filling my head.

"Dear God—" Instinctively, I pleaded for help. "Don't let Jeffrey suffer because I messed up. Please!"

Jeffrey moaned again. Blood still bubbled from the gash. I had to stop it. The thought came clearly. Laying him on the floor, I found a clean dishtowel in the kitchen. I covered the cut and pressed gently, then harder until the bleeding stopped. Tying the cloth in place, I sat back and let out a long breath.

Now what?

"His parents." I don't know where the words came from, but instinctively, I obeyed them. Hurrying to the phone table, I found the number they'd left, their cell phone. I dialed it and silently counted the rings. One, two, three—"Please answer," I pleaded—four, five—

"The mobile unit you are calling is not responding or is out of the area."

The recorded voice sent a wave of panic through me. What would I do now?

"God—"

My soft cry was interrupted by the recording. "At the tone, please leave a message."

A message. "M-Mr. and Mrs. Gilmore? This—this is Cindy. Jeffrey cut his arm. Could you meet us at the emergency room as soon as possible?"

Hanging up, I searched for the next step. I'd told them we'd be at the emergency room. At least I didn't have to call an ambulance. I'd driven Mom's station wagon. Digging the keys out of my purse, I half-carried Jeffrey in my arms to the car.

The two-mile trip seemed to take forever, but when I finally pushed through the doors, a wild relief rushed over me. We were there! A nurse stopped us, waving us over to a desk. "We have to fill in the admitting forms," she insisted. "Patient's name?"

"Jeffrey Gilmore."

"Address?"

When I didn't know the zip code, she raised an eyebrow. "I'm the sitter," I explained. The eyebrow lifted another half inch as she glanced at the boy in my arms. I wanted to sink through the floor, but I was still responsible for Jeffrey.

Lifting my chin, I told her, "I called his parents' cell phone and left a message."

"I'll need their permission to admit him," she said crisply. "Why don't I try their number again?" I gave it to her, and this time they must have answered. A moment later she was inputting information, asking about insurance, then finally hanging up. "They're just a few miles away," she explained, snapping the plastic admitting band around Jeffrey's wrist. "You'll stay with him until they arrive?"

I nodded, helping Jeffrey into the wheelchair an orderly had pushed up beside us. Silently, I walked beside it as they pushed him inside.

A doctor dressed in a pale green surgical suit strode in, peered at Jeffrey, then nodded. "You stopped the bleeding."

"I was a Girl Scout."

He smiled. "I thought they only sold cookies."

I stared at him, horrified. How could he joke?

His face sobered. "What happened?"

I explained about Jeffrey taunting me, pulling my hair, how I'd darted after him, about the storm door. "It's my fault, but I was so frustrated."

That's when Jeffrey's mother burst in. "My baby!" She ran toward him, but the doctor stopped her. "Watch the arm. It's not stitched up yet."

A minute later Mr. Gilmore arrived. It was getting pretty crowded, so I slipped out the door. I wanted to go home. More than anything I wanted to curl up in my bed and cry until I fell asleep. But I couldn't leave without knowing Jeffrey was all right. So I sat in the waiting room, staring at the wall, wishing I hadn't tried to grab Jeffrey, wishing I hadn't chased after him, wishing I hadn't locked the storm door, and praying that he'd be all right.

As I was sitting there, my head down, a shadow fell across my lap. I looked up at Mr. Gilmore. "I understand we have a lot to thank you for," he said quietly.

"Thank me for?" He had to be kidding.

"Dr. Lawrence explained what happened. He was quite impressed with how cool you were. He said that if you hadn't kept your cool, things could have been a lot more serious. So, thanks."

With a pat on the shoulder, he headed back inside. I couldn't believe he'd actually thanked me. And then I realized he should have been thanking God. He was the One who'd helped me put aside my panic and stay cool under fire. He had answered my prayers. He was with me the whole time. "Thank you, Lord," I quietly prayed.

We give thanks to you, O God, we give thanks, for your Name is near; men tell of your wonderful deeds.

Psalm 75:1

God Speaks:

Are you quick to turn to Me when you need help but slow to thank Me for all the good things I send your way?

> **If you listen to me whisper now, I won't have to shout later.**
>
> **—GOD**

Confessions of a Fat Girl

" **K**ristine—is that actually you?"

"You look incredible!"

I stood there and basked in it for a minute. You don't spend a whole summer eating salads without Thousand Island and not glow in the results just a little.

Ashley wrapped her fingers around my arm. "What made you do it? Did you just get tired of being fa—? How much weight did you lose?" Ashley squealed.

"About 20 pounds," I said. "I'm still working on it though."

"Don't lose another ounce," Desiree said. "You look amazing. And I'm not the only one who thinks so."

Ashley leaned in to shout over the roar of the crowd in the bleachers behind us. "It was Jason who told me to check out Kristine Westmore. He said you must have dumped fifty pounds—"

"But what do guys know about weight?" Desiree cut in again. "The point is, you have to come to the party at Ashley's after the game. Then he can really check you out!"

They both tossed their hair. I couldn't help it. I tossed mine too.

Ashley poked me. "So will you come?"

"Where's your house?" I asked.

Ashley gave my new figure one more approving once-over with her eyes. "You know Smokey Vista?"

Everyone knew Smokey Vista Drive. Driving a Porsche didn't get you as much clout as living on Smokey Vista.

"Why don't we meet right here at the gate after the game? You can go with us."

I'd already heard those words earlier that afternoon—from more familiar voices.

"You don't have a swimsuit with you, do you?" Ashley asked.

"Like she carries one in her purse!" Desiree said.

Ashley tossed again. "No problem. You can wear one of mine."

I like to think I remembered Caroline, Mikey, and Jen were going to meet me before I ran into the three of them at the gate. But if I'm honest with myself, I think I was actually peering into the crowd for Desiree and Ashley when Mikey blew his trumpet in my ear.

"The band geeks are here," Jen said. "Let the reveling begin!" Caroline was already unbuttoning the collar of her uniform. "We'll get changed, and then we can go to Round Table."

My mind was racing. These were my best friends, but how often did I get invited up to Smokey Vista Drive?

"Actually, there's a party," I said. "I was invited to Ashley Barrett's—"

"Oh, excuse me for living!"

"Did she ask to see your gold card?"

"Knock it off, you guys!" I said. "Ashley and Desiree invited me and—"

"Desiree too?" Mikey asked.

"I'm sure their invitation didn't include us," Jen said. "So if you're going to that party—we'll see you later."

Caroline tugged at the uniform buttons that gaped open over her stomach.

"Why don't you come with me?" I offered.

"No thanks. I prefer to hang out with people a little higher on the food chain."

"Was I like this last year?" I asked.

"Like what?"

"Putting down everybody who was different from us, being bitter because some people have it better?"

"Last year, you thought cheerleaders and football players and student council biggies were all a bunch of glory-seeking light-mongers. Now you're going to go party with them!"

"Don't you ever wonder if there's anything out there besides Round Table?"

"No, if you're talking about the cheerleader brain-trust. But if that's what you're looking for, knock yourself out."

When I arrived at the party, Jason appeared at my side in an instant. "You know what's like, so weird?" he began.

I shook my head—and tugged self-consciously at the bottoms of Ashley's hot pink two-piece.

"Usually after a game, I'm like, totally hyper. All I want to do is, like tear something up, ya' know what I'm saying?"

I didn't, but I nodded anyway. I was talking to the running back with the shoulders. He'd only been a number on a jersey to me until that night—and I'd been nothing to him.

"But right now," he went on, "all I want to do is sit here and talk to you. That's like, so weird."

"So are you going to introduce me, or are you going to be a jerk and keep her all to yourself?"

We both looked up at Ryan Mifflin, whose blue eyes were zoned in on me like two laser beams. I didn't point out that we had been in the same math classes since seventh grade and that an introduction was entirely unnecessary. I just stared back at him—and then down at my Diet Pepsi.

"Hey, loser," Ryan said, poking Jason with his bare toe. "Go get me another drink."

Ryan sat down and stuck out his hand. "Ryan Mifflin," he said.

"I know," I said.

"No, see actually, you don't." Ryan looked around and then leaned in. I adjusted the straps on the two-piece. "A lot of people think they know me because I let them think they do. But you know what's weird?"

I shook my head and got the oddest sensation of déjà vu as Ryan told me how much he really just felt like talking to me.

"You found one then," Ashley said to me, nodding approvingly at the big T-shirt I'd snagged from her dresser. She'd given me free reign when I'd told her I was cold. Actually, I just wasn't used to sitting around in something smaller than my underwear.

"You've got great legs," Desiree said. "Have you thought about trying out for cheerleading next year?"

"How about her?" Jason said. "Why don't you ask her to try out?"

We all followed his eyes to the glass doors that led from the house to the pool. Ryan was talking to a girl who had twenty pounds on anybody on the patio. I stifled a gasp.

"Who is that, anyway?" Ashley said.

I didn't answer, but I knew. It was Caroline.

"Ryan's going to mess with her mind."

Ryan had backed Caroline against the house and had his hand up on the wall over her head. Her face was expressionless—and bright red.

"Heaven only knows what he's saying to her," Desiree said.

"You ought to go stop him, Jason."

"No—check it out. He's got her going already."

Ashley slapped him, but she laughed. Me? I just stood there, frozen, not saying a word to defend my best friend.

"What's he doing now?" Ashley asked.

Caroline had slid out from under Ryan's arm and was backing away from him. Ryan bore down on her, moving her right toward the pool. I watched in horror as Caroline stepped backward into the water. I finally came unfrozen and bolted for poolside. Ashley caught my arm.

"I wouldn't," she whispered.

And I didn't.

At least I didn't until Caroline had hauled herself out with her T-shirt stuck to her skin, outlining every bulge and dimple. She'd already gotten to the door—and Ashley had already yelled, "Don't go in the house without drying off first!" when I finally shook off Ashley's hold and went to Caroline, with a towel.

"Here," I said to her.

She took the towel from me and covered her face with it as we both walked through the house for the front door.

"Do you get it now?" she said to me when we were outside. "These people are animals!"

"I'm sorry, Caroline."

"Why should you be sorry? You're not one of them—" She peered out at me from under the towel. "Are you?"

Something clicked in me—something I'd almost forgotten until then.

"That's not why I lost weight," I said. "I did it because of the temple thing."

"What temple thing?"

"How the Bible says your body's a temple of the Holy Spirit, and you shouldn't abuse it."

"You're seriously telling me you did it—"

"For God," I said.

She shook her head. "And did you team up with the beautiful people 'for God?'"

"I'll admit it—I got caught up in all the attention. And besides, you and Jen and Mikey were being so cynical and bitter."

"Excuse me for being real," Caroline said.

"Hey," I said. "Why did you decide to come anyway?"

"I thought you might need a friend," she said.

As I sat on Ashley's front curb waiting for my dad to come pick me up, I realized it was the first time that night I hadn't had some-body babbling in my ear. That's when my own voice started in.

Well, it said, *why did you bother with all the diet soda and bread sticks?* It really would be a bummer if the reason I'd lost weight was to get in with the "right" crowd. I'd truly been think-ing about my body being a temple of God's Spirit. And what had that gotten me?

Proof of Caroline's friendship for one thing. A warning that guys with big shoulders are not necessarily "to die for," for another. Plus a mental poke that said my friends and I had judged people by appearances, too, and then called it "being real."

The headlights of our Bronco appeared around the corner, and I stood up. That was going to require some heavy praying. But first maybe Dad would drop me off at Round Table. There were some people there who needed to hear this.

The LORD does not look at the things man looks at. Man looks at the outward appearance, but the LORD looks at the heart.

1 Samuel 16:7

God Speaks:

Are there people in your life whom you have judged because of how they look or dress? See people through My eyes.

Just say grace.

—GOD

Cutting Thoughts

"We leave in ten minutes!" my mom called from the kitchen, where she was packing a picnic lunch for our day at King's Island Amusement Park. My dad walked by my room, carrying the cooler.

"About ready?" he asked.

"I will be as soon as Amanda gets here," I said. I was trying to keep my mind on my morning devotions as I waited impatiently for my best friend to arrive. The words I read floated before my eyes but wouldn't sink into my brain.

Why isn't she ever on time? I wondered as I checked my watch again. *I purposely told her to be here fifteen minutes ago, so we wouldn't be held up. But did it work? Noooo!* If thoughts could kill, Amanda would have been mortally wounded about then.

After another minute, I snapped my Bible shut. I couldn't concentrate. I was getting angrier by the second, and I was ready to let Amanda have it with both barrels when she arrived.

The doorbell rang, and I hurried to answer the door. "You're late," I informed her. "We almost left without you."

"Sorry," Amanda apologized. "My mom made me clean my room before I left."

Poor excuse, I thought. *You should have kept your room clean in the first place. I do.* By my exacting standard of friendship, Amanda had just slipped another notch.

In fact, I was so irritated at my friend that as we drove to the park, I made a mental list of all the things about her that bugged me. While Amanda chattered away, my mind logged one cutting thought after another. Never on time was, of course, first on the list. That was quickly followed by too messy—her room looked like a bomb had gone off in it. From there I went to: talks too much, too giggly, and too opinionated. I threw in "impulsive" just to round things off.

By the time we got to King's Island, I was beginning to wonder why I'd invited Amanda to go and why she was my best friend. But I have to admit, once we got to the park, Amanda and I did have fun. As we waited in line for the rides, we used the time for our favorite pursuit—people watching.

We pointed out people with especially nice clothes and those with especially weird ones. I laughed at a boy with a mohawk, giggled at a guy covered with tattoos, and laughed out loud at two girls who had dyed their hair purple and then shaved half of it off. I really didn't think I was hurting anyone. I was people watching—with a few side comments.

After a morning of roller coasters, Amanda and I decided to try something tamer. We chose the ferris wheel. As we stood in line, we noticed a disabled boy and his sister in front of us. Neither Amanda nor I said a word. We both abided by the rule that people with physical or mental handicaps were never to be made fun of. Two teenaged boys who were also in front of us apparently hadn't heard of that rule.

"Hey, retard, where's your mommy?" they yelled in baby voices. "Don't you know you're too stupid to ride this by yourself?"

I saw the boy duck his head, as if to physically avoid the barbs thrown his way.

"Isn't his sister going to do anything?" Amanda asked.

I shook my head. "I don't think she's old enough to know what to do."

"Well, someone should tell them to stop."

No one did.

The barbs continued even as the ferris wheel was being loaded. Amanda and I were fuming as we climbed into our seats and pulled the bar over our legs.

"What if they follow him through the park all afternoon?" I asked as the ride began. "What if they won't leave him alone?" My questions brought a determined look to Amanda's face.

A couple of minutes later when the boy and his sister got off the ride, the two guys quickly followed, and the harassment started again. When our turn came to get off, Amanda grabbed my hand and pulled me after her.

Amanda caught up with them and put us between them and their victim. She pointed an angry finger at the troublemakers. "You leave him alone!" she yelled. "You have no right to make fun of him."

The boys looked at Amanda in shock. So did I. She was standing up for a perfect stranger.

"We were only having a little fun," one of them said as they turned to walk away.

But Amanda wasn't finished yet. "Just because someone is different than you are doesn't give you any right to be mean to him."

Though the boys waved her words away, they hit me with full force. I'd acted intolerably all morning—to people I didn't even know by making fun of them and to Amanda for not living up to my image of the perfect friend. If thoughts could kill, I'd be standing in a near-empty amusement park.

"Thank you," the sister said to Amanda as she took her brother's hand and led him away. "Thanks for helping."

Amanda and I found the nearest park bench and sat down. "That was quick thinking," I told her, realizing with a smile that I was complimenting her for her impulsiveness—something that only hours before I'd found fault with. "You were really brave to do that."

Amanda smiled.

"Be merciful, just as your Father is merciful."

Luke 6:36

God Speaks:

Just as I extend My grace to you, you are to extend grace to others.

If you must have the last word, make it "Sorry."
—GOD

Father's Day?

I 've heard it said that you always hurt the ones you love. In the past few years, that sure is the way it's been with me and my parents.

The first hurt came when my folks separated on the day I turned fifteen. "Happy birthday, Max. I'm leaving," my mom said as she packed her bags and walked out. Well, maybe it wasn't quite that cold, but it sure felt that way.

The second hurt was the divorce. The day I got my driver's license my dad shook my hand, handed me a set of car keys, and told me their court date had been set for later that week. It's like my parents purposely chose the major events in my life to spring their hurts on me.

Since the divorce, there's been one hurt after another. Some days my life feels like a game of "Let's use Max to get even with each other"—especially on my mom's part. Her latest hurt is enforcing visitation this weekend even though Sunday is Father's Day, and I had hoped she might let me spend it with Dad.

When my parents split, I chose to stay with my dad. Not just because of the guy thing, but because Dad and I are great friends. He's been my baseball coach, backyard-batting instructor, fishing buddy, driving teacher—we've always done everything together.

With Father's Day coming up, I asked Mom if I could be with her on a different weekend. She just said no. I think spending Father's Day with my mom is her latest way to make Dad's life miserable, while making me feel awful in the process. Sometimes my mom can be pretty hard to love.

With all this craziness going on, I did the only sane thing I knew to do. I called O'Brien.

Next to my dad, Tom O'Brien is my best friend. He's so much like me it's scary—same look (blond hair, brown eyes, 5'10", and skinny) and same thoughts on life's major issues—GMC trucks (for), girls (for), and God (definitely for). The one big way we're different is that O'Brien is more levelheaded than I am. So I called O'Brien and filled him in.

"Maybe she misses you and can't stand to be without you," he told me without the slightest hint of sarcasm.

"Did I dial the right number?" I asked him.

"Maybe she plans to take you shopping for a great Father's Day gift, and then she's going to bring you home so you can have all day Sunday with your dad."

"O'Brien, are you nuts?"

"Maybe she thinks this is another opportunity for payback time with your dad," O'Brien said, finally giving me the answer I wanted.

"Bingo!" I shouted. "But when is payback time going to end?"

"I think you need to ask her that," O'Brien replied.

So that night I took the phone into my room, so my dad wouldn't hear, and called my mom. I said a silent prayer as I dialed her number, *God, don't let me get her answering machine, and let her see things my way.*

God was only half listening.

My mom answered the phone, but things went downhill from there. Yes, she knew it was Father's Day weekend, but no she didn't understand why I couldn't spend time with her. She said I got to see Dad all the time and that she needed her time with me.

The longer my mom talked, the angrier I got. Before I hung up, I said some really hurtful things. "I don't want to spend time with you ever again let alone over Father's Day weekend!" was the last one I remember. I felt like every last little bit of love I had for my mom was gone—forever.

I stormed out of my room to find my dad and to see if he could fix things. I reminded him that Sunday was Father's Day and repeated my phone call with my mom as well as I could remember.

"Max," my dad said with a sigh, "as much as I'd like to spend Father's Day with you, it is your mom's weekend."

"But doesn't it make you angry?" I insisted.

"Angry?" he said. "No, it doesn't make me angry. It makes me sad. Sad that your mom still tries to hurt me through you. Sad that we've put you in the middle of all this. Sad that—"

I waved my hand at my dad and walked out of the room. I could see he wasn't going to help. *I'll plot my own revenge myself,* I decided.

I went to my room to think of ways to keep from spending the weekend with my mom. Even as I made my plans, I could hear O'Brien's voice saying, *Maybe she misses you so much she can't stand to be without you.*

While part of me wanted to tell that voice to shut up, another part of me listened. I thought O'Brien was kidding when he'd said that on the phone earlier, but I realized he wasn't.

Okay, maybe my mom was just as hurt by the divorce as Dad and I were. Sure, she had walked out, but that didn't mean her life was what she wanted it to be. And just because I felt like my mom was treating me badly didn't give me the right to treat her badly in return.

I was surprised at the direction my thoughts had taken. *God, sometimes I think You put O'Brien in my life to keep me from messing things up completely,* I thought.

As hard as it was going to be, I knew I had to call my mom back and apologize. I also knew I needed to try to explain to her how important it was for me to spend this weekend with Dad. Mostly though, I needed to tell her it was time to stop hurting the ones we love.

It will start with me, I decided. Right here. Right now.

If you are angry, don't sin by nursing your grudge. Don't let the sun go down with you still angry—get over it quickly.

Ephesians 4:26 TLB

God Speaks:

It takes a lot of courage to say, "I'm sorry." Learn to value your relationships more than you value being right.

Got questions? I'm the answer.

—GOD

Do You Ever Wonder?

It was a gray autumn day with a hint of rain in the air, and my best friend, Amy, and I were lying in her backyard as the leaves fell around us. We both had the hoods of our sweatshirts pulled up to keep ourselves warm, and Amy had promised me hot cider when her latest brainstorm was over. She wanted to see how many leaves we could catch. It was good luck to catch a falling leaf she had told me. I needed all the luck I could get, so here I was, lying on my back under the maple tree.

"Do you ever wonder how a leaf knows when to fall?" Amy asked as she stretched to catch a yellow leaf that floated just out of her reach. "Does it decide, 'I'm ready to take the plunge!' or is it hanging on for dear life until a big wind comes along and knocks it off its branch?"

"Amy, you're nuts." I told her. "Of course, I don't wonder about that."

"Well, do you ever wonder . . . ?"

I tuned Amy out. *What I wonder about,* I thought, *is how I'm going to get along without you. I like being backyard friends. I like sitting on the split-rail fence and being half in my yard and half in yours. I like the crazy ideas you have and being part of the adventures they lead to—like this one. What I wonder is what I'll do after you move.*

"I caught one!" Amy yelled, holding up her trophy—an orange and yellow maple leaf. "Try harder, Kelly!"

I put up my arms so Amy would think I was trying, but my heart wasn't in it. The wind blew, and leaves fell like rain. "I almost got another one!" Amy yelled. "How are you doing?" she asked me.

I sat up. "I'm cold, Amy. Can we go in?"

Amy sat up and waved her leaf. *One leaf—one day until Amy moves. That leaf isn't lucky at all,* I thought.

As Amy and I drank our cider, we talked about the years we'd been friends. From kindergarten through sophomore English, we'd been a team. We didn't think anything could separate us. Nothing could—until Amy's dad announced he was taking a job in another part of the state.

I could feel tears well up in my eyes again. I'd cried a lot that week. Amy had too. "It's not fair," I told her for the hundredth time. "We've been friends forever. Why did your dad have to take this job?"

Amy wiped her eyes. "I told you. Better pay. Great benefits. Dumb adult stuff."

"I don't ever want to grow up," I announced miserably.

That night, I thought about what I'd told Amy. "God, I know I should act like an adult about this, but I don't want to. I want to kick and scream and throw a tantrum until someone says Amy can stay."

Outside my window I could hear the rain start. "God, I feel like I'm caught in a storm, and I can't see You anymore. I want to believe this is for the best, but it doesn't feel that way."

Trust Me, the rain seemed to tap on the window. *Trust Me.*

The sound of the storm made me think of the Bible story where Peter jumped out of his boat and started walking across the water to Jesus. Peter was okay as long as he kept his eyes on Jesus, but when he focused on the storm going on around him— he sank. If Jesus hadn't reached out His hand, Peter would have gone under.

"Okay, God, maybe I'm focusing on the storm and not on You," I prayed, "but I doubt You can make anything good come of this. It's too hard to say good-bye to my best friend."

Watching Amy leave was every bit as hard as I thought it would be. Sure we promised to call each other, but we both knew things would never be the same. When Amy's car pulled away, I felt my heart break.

That weekend my dad told me he'd seen a moving van in front of Amy's old house. "I guess the new family's settling in." I didn't answer.

"Would you like to go say hello?" he asked.

"Not really," I said walking out the back door.

I thought I'd sit on the fence and mope, but when I got there, I was surprised to see a girl about my age lying in Amy's backyard, looking up at the trees. She sat up when she saw me. "Hi, I'm Rachel. We moved here from Florida," she said.

"I'm Kelly. I've lived here all my life," I told her.

"Lucky you," Rachel said as she lay back down. "These trees are great. All they have in Florida are palm trees."

"Yeah, but it's warm there this time of year," I said, pulling up the hood of my sweatshirt.

"Do you ever wonder how leaves know when to change color?" Rachel asked. "Do they say, 'I feel like wearing red today instead of green' and then just change? Do you ever wonder about that?"

I looked at Rachel in astonishment.

"Did I say something dumb?" Rachel asked. "You're looking at me funny."

"No, not at all," I said, climbing off the fence and going over to lie down beside her. "What I wonder is how a leaf knows when to fall off a tree. I mean does it decide, 'I'm ready to take the plunge!' or is it hanging on for dear life until a big wind comes along and knocks it off the branch?"

Rachel nodded.

As the two of us lay there, I thought about my prayer from the night before. *God, I wonder, is this the start of a beautiful friendship?*

Trust Me, came the answer whispered on the wind. *Trust Me.*

Trust in the LORD with all your heart and lean not on your own understanding.

Proverbs 3:5

God Speaks:

Exercise your faith by putting all your questions in My hands.

Planning for your
future? I am.

—GOD

Dreams

"What happened, Mandy?" Vicki asked, as she passed me in the hall behind the examining rooms.

I smoothed the Band-Aid over my arm and winced. "Another scratch," I said. "My fourth this week."

"You have to watch those killer cats," she said. "Although if I stopped to do first aid every time a patient got me, I'd be here at the medicine cabinet half the day."

It was her way of telling me to stop being a wimp and get back to work, and I was about to when she popped her head back around the corner and added, "There's a phone call for you. Line 2. And then get the Callahans and Muffin into D."

Yea, I said to myself, *I love Muffin and the Callahans. Last time they brought that mutt in here, I had to wrestle her to the floor just so Dr. Knowles could listen to her heartbeat.*

I was still mumbling when I picked up the phone and punched Line 2.

"What?" Chad said on the other end.

"What?" I shouted back from mine. It was practically impossible to have a conversation with fifteen dogs yapping twenty feet away. "Talk fast—I have to get back to work."

"There's an opening down here," Chad said.

"At the theater?"

"Yeah—one of the stagehands has to quit, and they need somebody starting next week. The pay's lousy—"

"But it doesn't matter," I finished for him. Any of us drama club maniacs would have paid them to let us work at the summer stock theater.

"I told them about your tech work at Webster High," Chad said, "and they were impressed. I told them you were almost as good as I am."

Behind me, Vicki was tapping her pencil on the counter, and beyond her in the waiting room, Muffin was chewing up a magazine while the Callahans looked on.

"What do I do?" I hissed at Chad.

"Call this number—by Saturday."

I scratched the number on the back of a heartworms pamphlet and stuffed it into my pocket.

"Muffin, Room D," Vicki said curtly.

I barely heard her. I was busy thinking. *There might actually be a way out of this zoo.*

"It's the perfect opportunity for you," my dad had said the day he told me he'd gotten me a job at the veterinary hospital. "You've always wanted to be a vet, so this will give you a chance to work in the business for the summer."

The truth was—I hadn't had that dream since I was about twelve and certainly not since I'd gotten involved in the theater at school. I'd never gotten a high from looking down some cocker spaniel's throat the way I did running a light board and painting scenery.

But Dad had watched me ride our horses and groom them and feed them since I was six, and—bingo—I was shoving pills down the throats of cats who would shred me to ribbons if given the chance. Grooming my own horses was one thing. Playing "keep-away" with Dobermans all day was another.

When I got home that night, Dad was leaning against the fence on the west corral, observing Lolly, our chestnut mare.

"Look at this gal, Mandy," he said. "She's absolutely square."

"You think she'll foal this weekend?" I asked.

"Oh, yeah, I'll be waking you up. They always deliver in the middle of the night."

I looked at poor, miserable Lolly. I'd helped bring her first colt into the world. It had been cool, I had to admit, but did I want to do that—for the rest of my life?

I shook my head. "Chad called me today," I said. "He says they have an opening at the summer stock theater for a stagehand—"

"He's a fool to take a job like that," Dad said. "They don't pay half what you're making, and it won't prepare him for his future. What does he want to do when he's out of school?"

"Dad, he already works—"

"I'm proud of you," he said. "You've got your head on straight. You know what you want, and you're going after it. The money you're making with Knowles is really going to help out with college."

He had the whole conversation started, discussed, and finished before he even knew what it was about.

"You have a God-given gift for working with animals," he said. "I'm glad to see you using it."

"Feeding people's house pets isn't exactly using it, Dad," I said. "I haven't touched a horse since I've been there, and besides, I don't—"

"I'll talk to Knowles," he said. "Come on. Let's get these horses fed."

My father and Dr. Knowles go way back to veterinary school. Dad never finished because his father died, and he had to keep the family's feed store on its feet until he could sell it. Somehow he never did sell it.

He and Dr. Knowles were still good friends, which is probably why when I got to work the next morning Vicki scowled at me and said, "You're going out on a ranch call with the doctor today."

"He colicked," Mr. Crowley told us, stroking his mahogany-colored gelding's mane.

Dr. Knowles ran a hand down Sultan's forelock. "Get some sand in your belly, old buddy?"

"He wants to roll," said Crowley. He looked at me. "That could be fatal."

I knew that. A horse will roll on the ground to try to eliminate the severe pain in its stomach and end up twisting its insides irreversibly and dying.

"You want me to walk him?" I asked Dr. Knowles.

He nodded. "Listen for bowel sounds. I'll mix up some bran and Metamucil."

Fabulous. I could be up in the first beam right now, focusing a state-of-the-art lighting instrument—and here I was listening for bowel sounds.

But I'd done it enough times with our seven horses to know I was possibly saving the animal's life, and that was nice. Besides, I had everybody giving me all these chances in a field where a lot of people, like Vicki, didn't get past the phone and the thermometers. I was fortunate. My parents were willing to pay for most of my education, and I earned enough money in my job to handle the rest myself.

It couldn't have been much after 4:00 A.M. when my dad woke me the next morning. Lolly was about to deliver.

By the time I got to the barn, the feet had already poked their way into the world, and within twenty minutes, the rest of a gooey little filly was lying in the hay next to her mother.

"Well, look here, Lolly," Dad crooned. "You've got you a beautiful little girl."

As my father watched the newborn foal lift her head then begin to try to stand up, his face was actually glowing. I was going through the motions as I had so many times before. For my father, this was a miracle. For me, it was just a job.

That's when it occurred to me that my working at the animal hospital, preparing for a career as a veterinarian, was the spinning out of his dream not mine. If I didn't feel the joy of it, I was cheating him as much as I was myself.

I shoved my hands into my jeans pockets as I watched him, and my fingers curled around the heartworms pamphlet. It was Saturday, and the phone number for the theater was right there at my fingertips.

"There she goes!" Dad cried.

Lolly's foal was gathering her legs under herself. With one courageous heave, she went up on her feet—and fell flat on her homely little nose.

I may fall on my face, too, I thought, but I need to at least try to sort this out.

"Dad," I said, "you believe in dreams don't you?"

My father didn't even blink. "You bet I do," he said, nodding at Lolly's baby. "Here's one come true, right here."

I sighed a huge breath and plopped myself down in the hay. "Then, Dad," I began, "can we talk?"

No eye has seen, no ear has heard, no mind has conceived what God has prepared for those who love him.

1 Corinthians 2:9

God Speaks:

Put your dreams in My hands. I'm in the business of making dreams come true.

Are you talking to me?
—GOD

Fly Talk

Grandpa Filbert talks to flies—the fishing kind. Of course, he also talks to God—right out loud and not just when he's praying before a meal.

I used to, when I was younger. Talk to God, I mean. But it's hard talking to someone who doesn't talk back. So even though I still believed in Him, I'd pretty much quit praying or thinking about praying.

The summer I turned fifteen, my cousin Jake and I stayed with Grandpa. Mostly, we fixed up the riverfront, but we fished, too. One hot August afternoon, Grandpa said he'd been talking to the flies and learned that the trout were biting in the canyon.

I nodded, but I didn't need the flies to tell me that. The canyon walls cast long shadows over the water, shadows that trout like.

Behind me, Jake dangled his legs in the river as he tossed a baseball into his glove again and again. "It's too hot," he grumbled over the steady smack . . . smack . . . smack of the ball hitting leather. "But you go ahead, Evan," he told me, nodding upstream.

Grandpa threw his waders over his shoulder. I don't mind the cold water swirling around my knees, so I just put on my old tennis shoes and grabbed my rod. Ten minutes later, we stepped into the shadows of the cliffs.

According to Grandpa, the fish were hungry for mayflies, but after fifteen minutes, neither of us had had a bite.

"Those flies have never lied to me," Grandpa muttered.

"Maybe the fish lied to the flies," I offered, dodging away as he swatted me with his old hat, which had at least two dozen flies clinging to the band. He was still laughing as he sloshed through the water in his waders. "I'll try up by those rocks," he said, pointing toward the mouth of the canyon. The fish like to school downstream, where the rocks break the rush of the current. I picked the bottom of the rapids where the river spills out of the canyon. I'd hooked a brown there a couple days before.

Willows on the bank cast long shadows over the river, and I kept myself hidden in them as I waded into the water. The current tugged at my legs as I cocked my arm and cast my fly upstream. It lit on the water, then floated past me.

I was gathering in my line for another cast when I heard a shout. Looking upstream, I saw Grandpa leaning back, his rod bent like a rainbow. He had a big one, all right. A whop—

His rod whipped up straight as his line snapped. Without that big fish to pull against, Grandpa staggered back. Tossing my rod onto the bank, I tried to rush upstream, willow branches blocking my path.

"Ahhh!" Grandpa's hoarse cry echoed up the canyon walls as he fell.

"Grandpa!" His chest slid under the surface and water gushed into his waders. The current caught him, dragging him along. The weight of his waders made him clumsy. He pushed to his feet, but the river swept his legs away.

I knew I had to help him—had to stop him before the river banged him into a sharp rock or the weight of those waders dragged him down like an anchor. But he was already ten feet from shore. Even if I could have reached him, I wondered how I could hold on against the current.

A willow branch poked at my ear, and I pushed it away, then glanced at the tree. Long branches stretched six, maybe eight feet out over the water. Grabbing one of them, I yanked hard. It bent but didn't break.

When Grandpa was nearly in front of me, splashing out into the river, I grabbed a willow branch and stretched my other arm toward him. "Grandpa!" I yelled.

He reached for me and caught my hand but if only for a second. Then the current whirled him around. His weight yanked hard on my arm. My fingers slipped.

"No!" I screamed. My free arm thrashed through the water, snagging the suspenders of his waders. The river pulled at him, and the straps bit into my fingers, but I wouldn't let go.

"Safe," I gasped. For the moment. The problem was, I didn't know what to do next. My arms were stretched wide, one holding on to Grandpa, the other grasping the tree branch. "Can you stand up?"

"Twisted my knee," Grandpa gasped.

I groaned. With a bad knee and full waders, I knew he'd never be able to stand against the current, but I let go to help him, we both would be swept away.

The current tugged at Grandpa, stretching my arms like a rubber band. Pinpricks of pain darted up and down my arms. The water that had cooled my legs felt cold on my chest.

Grandpa moaned, "Lord, help me—" His eyes sagged shut, and I shuddered. Focusing on the bright colors of his hat, I tried to block out the pain, but I couldn't hold on much longer.

"Stupid flies," I muttered. "Why can't they really talk?"

Maybe they can. The words came from nowhere, filling my head, and then I remembered Jake sitting on the riverbank, his feet dangling in the water.

"Maybe they can," I whispered, echoing the silent thought.

"Grandpa," I called. His eyes fluttered open. "Your hat. Throw it in the water!" I was getting ready to explain, to convince him, but he just did it, weakly swatting at his hat once, twice—. By the time he hit the brim, his eyes had drooped shut again. The hat toppled forward and onto the water. It bobbed for a moment, a gaudy boat with colored feathers circling the brim, before the current swept it away.

My teeth chattered, and my arms burned with pain. Twice I twisted my wrist to read my watch, but only two minutes had passed, and I quit looking at it. I just hung on and hoped and prayed.

Finally, I heard the crunching of bushes downstream. "Help!" I shouted, as the cold water squeezed the air from my chest.

"Evan?" It was Jake's voice. A moment later, he pushed through the brush and rushed into the water. Holding on to the branch with me, he reached out and grabbed Grandpa's suspenders. Between the two of us, we pulled him to shore. Jake went back for help, and an hour later we were both wearing dry clothes, and the doctor was taping Grandpa's knee.

"Stay off your feet a couple days," he warned, frowning to make sure Grandpa obeyed. Then we were alone, just the three of us. Grandpa sighed.

"I don't mind telling you two, I was getting a mite worried," Grandpa murmured. "How is it you happened to check up on us, Jake?"

"This drifted past me," he explained, holding out grandpa's old hat. "You never let it out of your sight, so I figured you were in trouble."

There was a twinkle in Grandpa's eyes as he slapped the old hat back on his head. "That was right smart thinking, Evan, letting those flies do your talking."

I laughed, but I knew the idea hadn't come from me. But where? A stillness had settled over me amid the rushing current. Maybe God did talk to us. Maybe I just had to listen more carefully and learn to recognize His voice.

"The flies weren't the only ones talking," I whispered to Grandpa. He smiled. I think he understood.

Whether you turn to the right or to the left, your ears will hear a voice behind you, saying, "This is the way; walk in it."

Isaiah 30:21

God Speaks:

If you want to hear Me speak, you must be willing to listen.

Some things break my heart too.

—GOD

Growing Up in the Rain Forest

"I understand why you don't think I'm serious about this," I said to my dad. "I don't usually hang with things forever—"

"Colleen, you don't 'hang' with them long enough for me to pay for the equipment. We have Nordic skis, a racquetball racket, and two pairs of tap shoes."

"Sports are my connection with life. I want to try everything. Besides, that was when I was a kid. I've matured."

Dad closed his eyes as he leaned back in his seat. "That remains to be seen," he said. "Meanwhile, I'm going to hold off on buying you a jet ski. Wake me up when we get to Cuzco."

Within seconds he was whistling snores, and I was left watching Brazil disappear through the plane window and wondering why we were on our way to Peru to "rough it" when I would have been content finishing our vacation with my mother and little sister in Rio de Janeiro. But Dad said I "needed" to come with him.

I sighed. If I had any hope of wrangling the bucks for a jet ski when we got home, it was going to be in showing "maturity" on this little jaunt with Dad.

"How much farther?" I whined.

Dad turned around and glared at me, but Gabriella, our guide, smiled and said, "About another two minutes. Our boat is moored just up ahead on the bank of the Alto Madre de Dios River."

I groaned. "Then how long?"

"It's about a four-and-a-half-hour trip on the river—then we'll take a twenty-minute walk along a forest path to the edge of Cocha Juarez. There's a dock where we'll catch a catamaran. From there it's only a fifteen-minute paddle to Manu Lodge."

The only reason I was glad to get to the thatch-roofed Manu Lodge was that there were two beds in our room. I flopped down on one of them and fell into a coma until Dad woke me for dinner.

"Where's the bathroom?" I asked.

"Screened-in building," he said. "They like to keep it separate from the lodge."

Once I got there, it was easy to see—or smell why. The so-called bathroom was nothing more than a raised box with a toilet seat, located over a pit. I sank down on the steps to the latrine building and buried my face in my hands. I was supposed to spend three days here? My father still hadn't explained why.

"Hello," said a soft voice.

I jolted my head up to see Gabriella.

"Are you ill?" she asked.

I shook my head. "Not physically," I said.

"I get the feeling," she said in her gentle accent, "that you aren't happy about our hike into the rain forest tomorrow."

I could feel my mouth dropping open. "We're going in there?"

She nodded. "This is a tropical, moist forest, so you're likely to see, oh, maybe a hundred macaws, several species of primates. If we're lucky, we'll spot an emperor tamarin."

"Are we talking monkeys, here?"

"They usually mind their own business if we mind ours. You're in a reserve here. Scientists come from all over the world to study because it's very possible that by the next century any rain forest not protected by a conservation association will be destroyed by ranchers and farmers and loggers."

Am I supposed to be worried about that? I wondered. *Surely the world could go on without a few monkeys and parrots?*

"I think you're going to fall in love tomorrow," she said.

The next morning, Gabriella led us down a trail that left all sunlight behind. Above us were nothing but looping, twisting, climbing vines, forming a canopy with the trees.

"Do you see those deep marks on the bark?" Gabriella asked. "That's where a jaguar has been sharpening its claws."

I shuddered and then froze on the trail. A deafening roar filled the giant tree-domed room. I flung myself at my father.

"Congratulations!" Gabriella said. "You've heard your first howler monkey!"

"Cool," I said through my teeth.

My father threw his head back and laughed. Jet ski or no jet ski, I was getting more and more frustrated with the man. Why had he brought me here?

That's about the time it started to happen. I'm not sure how exactly. It might have been when we saw this mass of bright red flowers with these adorable little birds sticking their beaks into them, wings fluttering so quickly you couldn't even see them.

"Hummingbirds," Gabriella whispered to me.

Or it might have been the leaf mimic butterflies gathered at a puddle. It could even have been the emerald-green parrot blinking at us from over the glob of fruit it was having for lunch or the bright blue frog that clung to a shivering leaf as we passed.

But I do know what clinched it—

Gabriella stopped suddenly beside me and pointed to the canopy above us. Way up there, almost to the very top, a skinny black form with a tail as long as my leg let go of its tree with one arm and grabbed the next tree with its other one. I watched as the monkey swung again and again, almost in a circle above us.

"Spider monkeys," Gabriella said softly. "See how Mama hangs on with her tail while she grabs some fruit?"

No sooner had it registered that there were two junior spiders clinging to "Mama" when something small and black tumbled away from her and bounced against the tall tree trunk. I gasped as a baby spider monkey lodged in a branch not three feet from my elbow.

"Colleen, don't move!" Gabriella said.

I could hear my father's footsteps stop several yards behind me. It seemed as if both of them were miles away as I looked into the terrified eyes of a practically bald little being. It opened its pink mouth and stuck its whole paw in it. From out of the cracks came a frightened, high-pitched scream.

"Don't touch it," Gabriella whispered. "Here comes Mama— and she's not happy."

Just above me, the screeching mother spider monkey crashed toward her baby, with the other one still hanging on like superglue.

"Back away slowly," Gabriella whispered.

I tried, but when Mama got to Baby and snatched him up against herself, she turned her eyes on me, and I couldn't move. All I could do was look at her face, which was protective and scared and indignant all at the same time.

"It's okay," I said to her. "We won't hurt you or your babies. It's your forest."

She cocked her head at me, and for an instant our gazes were locked. Then with one last warning chitter she leaped up the tree and disappeared.

The next day, we took another boat—made of two dugout canoes—down the river, and for a while, I gurgled over the jaguar tracks on the bank and yet another species of outrageously colored bird on a branch. But after a couple of hours, I noticed the scenery changing. The thick forests dropped behind us, and the land on both sides of the river turned dry and brown, spiked only here and there with lifeless gray trees.

"What happened to the forest?" I asked.

"Cattle ranching mostly," Gabriella said sadly. "And some farming. The government borrows millions from the World Bank for developing those industries. They destroy the forests to do it, but then the soil erodes, and they can't grow crops or graze cattle there after a few years."

"It's a wasteland!" I said. "It's ugly!"

Gabriella shook her head. "That's not the worst of it. Destroying the forests means rubber tappers can't tap. The world's weather changes. We make the greenhouse effect worse. It endangers native cultures and keeps us from getting to lifesaving medicines. Obviously some animals are becoming extinct." She looked full at me. "Like your monkeys, Colleen."

I scowled at the skeleton trees. "Somebody needs to stop them!" I said.

"Somebody's trying," Gabriella said. "Even kids, younger than you. They'll raise money and buy an acre at a time, so it can be protected."

"How much?" Dad said.

"A hundred dollars an acre," she sighed.

"I want to go back to the rain forest," I said as we settled into our seats for the flight back home. "I'm telling you, Dad, that mother primate understood me. We connected."

My father groaned and adjusted his seat belt. "Colleen, if I hear this monkey bonding story one more time, I may change my mind."

"It was symbolic of the whole experience—change your mind about what?" I asked.

"The jet ski," he said. "I watched you grow up in Peru. I finally saw you appreciate something beyond what's fun for the moment. We'll price them when we get home."

I expected to feel some kind of thrill as I looked out the window and to dream of winging across the waves. But I felt something else—because of what I saw below.

Gabriella had said I'd see it when I flew back to Brazil—mile after mile of naked ground, where there should have been a jade-colored canopy. Useless land instead of a thriving rain forest, where jaguars could sharpen their claws and monkeys could—

Suddenly there was a huge lump in my throat. Had a mother monkey once swung from trees there? What had she done when they were cut down and hauled away? Had she looked imploringly into the eyes of the loggers and ranchers and farmers as she had into mine?

And had they cared?

I guess that's when I knew why I'd fallen in love with the forest—why the monkeys had done it for me. The rain forest was our connection with life—with the earth God had given us. I looked at my sleeping father, and a light went on in my head. That was why he'd taken me there in the first place.

I jiggled his arm. "Forget the jet ski," I said. "Let's buy a few acres instead."

He opened his eyes. "How long is this going to last?" he asked, grinning. But I think he knew I was going to hang with this one—forever.

The earth is the LORD's, and everything in it, the world, and all who live in it.

Psalm 24:1

God Speaks:

When you fail to appreciate what I have provided, you also fail to appreciate Me!

Feeling down? Just look up.

—GOD

The Hurting Hearts Club

The Hurting-Hearts Club wasn't an official club—not like the ones our school had for ecology or yearbook or band. There wasn't a sign posted on any bulletin board telling people where or when to meet. There were no bylaws, no dues, and there were only three members—DeeAnn, Beth, and I—all with broken hearts.

It was because of DeeAnn's breakup with her boyfriend, Craig, that the club started. "I know I've been out of the picture for a while, but I really need you guys," DeeAnn said when she showed up at our locker that afternoon. Beth and I grabbed her for a group hug.

"Gwen, can I come over this afternoon to talk?" DeeAnn asked.

"Sure, Dee-Dee," I said reverting to the name I'd used for her when we were little. "Beth and I usually go to my house after school." DeeAnn nodded. She didn't have to ask why we went there and not to Beth's. Over the years, she'd run into Beth's alcoholic father on several occasions. None of those meetings had been pleasant.

The last meeting had been more than two years before when Beth's mom had planned a surprise party for Beth's thirteenth birthday, and her father—even after all his promises—had shown up drunk. He said he'd gone out to have a beer to celebrate his daughter turning thirteen. I think he must have had one for every year of her life. What a present! Beth was a natural for club membership.

I was too. My parents had been separated for two months and were talking about a divorce. Mom kept herself busy at work, and I only saw Dad on the weekends, so I practically had the house to myself. Having Beth over had always helped fill up the emptiness.

That day was the first meeting of what came to be known as the Hurting-Hearts Club. At first all we did was sit around and gripe. Except for Beth. She was quiet most of the time, unless she had something important to say. Then DeeAnn and I knew we should listen.

Usually though, DeeAnn would gripe about Craig and what a creep he was, and I would gripe about my parents and how they didn't know how much they were hurting me, and Beth would just sit there.

That is, until one afternoon when the three of us had just settled ourselves in my room, and Beth burst out, "Why does God let stuff like this happen?" I was surprised at the anger in her voice. "Doesn't He care about us? Doesn't He know how much it hurts?"

Beth's questions were like arrows of anger and doubt that she shot up to Heaven. The arrows fell short of their mark and returned to earth, stinging the three of us with pointed questions we weren't sure how to answer.

Even though we all were Christians, none of us had ever asked God why our lives were so messed up. Until then.

We all were quiet for a minute. Then DeeAnn spoke up. "I guess if we really want the answer to that question, we need to ask God."

Beth and I looked at our friend as if she'd flipped. "And how do we do that?" I asked.

"I think we need to look it up in the Bible. After all, people say the Bible is how God speaks to us," DeeAnn offered.

"Do you know it well enough to find some answers?" Beth asked.

"Ummm," DeeAnn blushed, "not as well as I'd like but well enough to start looking. I think."

We all laughed at her honesty.

I went over and got my Bible out of my desk drawer. I used it on Sundays, but other than that, it stayed in the drawer. I never thought it might have some answers for my hurting heart.

It took us most of the afternoon and quite a few meetings after that, but we did find out some really helpful things.

That first day, we learned that God lets it rain on the just and the unjust. (See Matthew 5:45.) Even though the three of us loved God, it didn't mean we were immune to life's problems.

We also found, though, that God promises He won't give us more than we can handle in terms of problems or temptations. (See 1 Corinthians 10:13.) "I can see that in my own life," I said quietly after DeeAnn read the verse. "At least my mom and dad are just separated right now. That gives me hope they might still work through their problems. If they do end up getting a divorce, I'm sure God will give me the strength to handle it when that time comes."

In the next few days, we found some really positive things to hang on to. Of course, some of the things we already knew, but it was good to be reminded of the good stuff that's in the Bible.

"Breaking up with Craig still hurts," DeeAnn said, "but it helps to know God loves me more than Craig ever could."

Beth nodded. "I know I need to keep praying for my dad and his recovery, but until that happens, I'm thankful I have a Heavenly Father who can take his place."

"I know God doesn't want divorce," I said quietly, "and I know my parents know that too. Maybe it's time we all started believing God can heal their broken marriage."

"That's it!" DeeAnn exclaimed. "Our new name."

"What new name?" Beth asked.

"Well, we can't be the Hurting-Hearts Club anymore. It doesn't fit. So how about the Healing-Hearts Club?"

Beth and I laughed and agreed that the new name fit. After all, hadn't we found the best way to heal a hurting heart was God?

The LORD is my strength and my shield;
My heart trusted in Him, and I am helped;
Therefore my heart greatly rejoices.

Psalm 28:7 NKJV

God Speaks:

I know when you are hurting, and I truly understand.

"Big Bang Theory"?
You've got to be kidding.
—GOD

In the Shadow of the Moon

Randall hated girls—at least in science class. He'd made that perfectly clear when he had to dissect a frog with my friend Elizabeth last year.

"Just try not to throw up on the tray," he ordered, grabbing the scalpel from her hand.

The only thing he hated worse was Christians in science class. If you didn't believe in evolution, he figured you were practically illiterate. So I was not exactly thrilled to find him in my fifth-period science class. But I was totally bummed when Mrs. Emory posted the list of partners for our first project.

Solar Eclipse: Randall Martin and Valerie Willis

I headed for her desk, but Randall beat me to it. "Mrs. Emory, there is no way—"

"I'm not going to start changing partners," she cut in smoothly. "You'll just have to make the best of it, Randall." The look she gave me said that went for me too. Sighing, I wished I'd signed up for French instead.

Scooting my chair over to his desk, I flipped open my notebook. We had one week to make a model of a solar eclipse. "I can check out some books from the library," I offered.

He snorted. "Who needs books? Eclipses are simple. You get a big cardboard box. I'll take care of the rest."

"Randall, we're supposed to work as a team."

"Don't worry, Valerie." He made my name sound like a sneer. "I'll put your name on it too."

"That's not fair!"

"What do you care? You'll get an A out of it." He shrugged. "You don't believe any of this stuff anyway."

I shook my head. How could I explain that God and science weren't opposites? "OK," I said, "I'll get the box. But we're going to build it together."

The bell rang before he could object. Shoving my chair back under my desk, I grabbed my books and rushed out. It was going to be a long year.

That night, I added "solar eclipse" to my prayer list. "God, give me patience. And courage," I added, certain I'd need it. Funny thing was, I never thought to pray for Randall.

We met at my house. Even Randall could see that was easier than hauling the box around. He unpacked a light bulb on a clamp, a pad of paper, a small ball, and some clay.

"Have you got a wire coat hanger?" he asked, pulling open a pocketknife.

By the time I found a hanger in Dad's closet, Randall had cut a circle in one end of the box. The light was clamped on the top edge so it hung down and shone through the hole, lighting up the inside.

"The sun," he announced.

"I want to help too," I insisted.

"You just did." He waved the hanger at me.

"Randall!"

"OK, OK." He rolled his eyes. "Cut out a big circle of paper."

"Why?"

"Because the earth is round."

Patience, I muttered to myself, glad God heard even silent prayers.

While I drew around a dinner plate and cut out the circle, Randall bent the wire hanger back and forth breaking off a piece. He pushed one end into the ball and stuck the other into a clump of clay stuck on the bottom of the box.

"The moon," he announced. Snatching the paper from my hand, he taped it inside the box, across from the light. "Finito!"

I frowned. "Where's the eclipse?"

"Right—" He glanced at the circle of paper and frowned. Then he looked relieved and gave a quick nod. "I just got the moon in the wrong place."

"The wrong place? Randall, you can't just move the moon anywhere you want to."

"I'm not moving it just anywhere." Suddenly he sounded very serious. He must have thought his reputation as a science whiz was on the line because instead of brushing me off, he explained carefully. "The sun is about four hundred times bigger than the moon, but it's also four hundred times farther away. That means they look about the same size from the earth, so when the moon passes directly between the earth and the sun, it exactly covers the sun."

I watched as he peeled the clay off the bottom of the box and moved the ball closer to our paper earth. The two faint shadow circles it made on the paper swept closer and closer together until they crossed.

"That's the spot," he announced, pressing the clay down hard to hold our moon in place. "The dark shadow where they cross is a total eclipse. The land under the lighter shadows isn't exactly in line with the moon and the sun, so the moon only blocks out part of the sun. The people there see a partial eclipse." The old cockiness was back, an I-told-you-so tone that felt like fingernails on a blackboard. But I shook it off, trying to catch hold of a thought.

"Randall, what would happen if the moon were smaller?"

He shrugged. "If it were smaller or farther away, it wouldn't completely cover the sun. We'd only have partial eclipses, or if it were small enough, we might not notice them at all."

I nodded slowly. "And what if the moon were bigger? Or closer?" I added, even though I'd already figured out the answer.

"Eclipses would be a lot more common." He sounded bored as he started gathering up the bits of paper and cardboard.

"The moon's orbit—" I was grinning now. "Randall, what about the orbit? What if the moon went around the north and south poles instead of near the equator?"

He frowned for a second. "I guess there wouldn't be any eclipses at all."

I laughed. "Don't you see? A solar eclipse is one of the most awesome things on earth, but we only have them because the moon is the right size in the right place, going around in the right orbit."

Randall shrugged. "Yeah. What a coincidence."

"Coincidence?" A silence settled between us. "What are the odds, Randall? If an uncontrolled explosion made the universe, what are the odds that the right amount of matter came together at the right distance from the earth and in the right orbit so that we could be awed by a solar eclipse?"

I could almost see the numbers flashing in front of his eyes as he tried to estimate what the chances were. Finally, he shook his head. "They're pretty incredible."

I didn't say anything. Randall had pretty much said it all. But I knew I'd just seen God's hand in the shadow of the moon. Maybe Randall had seen it too.

Through him all things were made; without him nothing was made that has been made.

John 1:3

God Speaks:

There is a lot of debate about how the world was created. The most important question is not "How" but "Who."

It's Your Turn

"**H**ey," I said. "Double tomorrow night?"

"Yep."

"Meet you guys at the beach?"

"Yep."

"I can pick Bree up in your truck?"

"No strippin' the gears."

"Nope."

I could feel Jake's big, sloppy, slow grin easing through the phone. "It's always a blast."

"This is your third party. You're getting to be like a regular member at youth group."

"Yep," he said, "but the next time it's your turn."

"Yep," I said automatically.

But when I hung up the phone, I looked down at Duke. A vague uneasiness nudged at me.

"What do you think he meant by that?" I asked. "You don't think 'my turn' means he wants me to go to one of his parties?"

Duke didn't answer. OK, he's an Irish setter—he never says much.

Just then the phone rang, and I dove for it.

"Hi, Todd," Bree said softly from the other end.

"Hi," I said.

There was a husky pause—the kind that replaces "How are you?" and "What are you doing?" because you think you know each other so well you don't need to say that stuff. Bree broke into it first.

"I just talked to Erin. She says you guys want to double tomorrow night."

Erin was Jake's girlfriend. She reminded me of a TV news reporter going after a fast-breaking story. It couldn't have been five minutes since I'd talked to Jake, and she already had our conversation on the air.

"Do you mind if we go out with them?" I asked.

"No. But we're not going to one of their parties, are we?

I almost choked.

"No," I said. "Why?"

"Erin said something about Jake thinking it was time you gave his friends a chance since he's always doing stuff with our youth group."

"You wouldn't feel comfortable with that, huh?" I said.

"I wouldn't go! You know what those parties are like—heavy metal blasting out the windows, people drinking everywhere you look. I mean, there might even be some pot—"

"OK, OK, then we won't ever go!"

My voice came out sharper than I'd wanted it to. Even Duke took his tennis ball and retreated under my desk with it.

"You don't have to yell," Bree said. I could almost see her doing the stress pull through her hair with her hand.

"I'm sorry," I said. "Look—tomorrow night's gonna be a blast—" It took me awhile to get the softness back in her voice. And I didn't feel a whole lot better when I hung up. Duke lunged out from under the desk and pushed the tennis ball at me. Absently I pushed it away.

The slobbery ball dropped in my lap. I slapped it away.

By Friday, I had stopped mulling over the problem. After all, I decided, it wasn't even a problem yet. Jake would probably forget about it anyway.

Besides, I knew as Bree and I drove up to Crescent Beach in Jake's truck that the night was going to be a blast. She was sitting next to me so Duke could ride shotgun. When I turned off the ignition, he rolled his tongue over her head, dripping slobber into her hair.

Jake and Erin were already at the party when we arrived. In fact, Jake had helped build the fire, consumed four hot dogs, and was now chasing Erin down the beach.

"We'll catch him later," I said to Bree. "Want to go for a walk?"

"Sure," Duke's tail said, and he tore off down the beach.

Bree automatically tucked her hand inside mine, and we strolled after Duke. The sun was just melting into the ocean, cutting a black silhouette out of the cliff ahead of us. Bree stopped.

"What?" I asked.

"Would you look at that."

Bree laughed and pointed to where Jake was chasing Erin, beating on his chest and hollering like a gorilla. "I hope he doesn't teach you that," she said.

Erin got to us first, squealing and hiding behind Bree. Jake caught her in a headlock.

"You're such a romantic, Jake," Bree said dryly. "You really ought to lighten up on the hearts and flowers, you know."

"Me and Erin are going swimming," Jake said. "You guys want to come?"

"No," we said simultaneously. But I could feel myself grinning as he tore off his T-shirt and kicked into the water.

We finally did get Erin and Jake to sit down when the party was almost over, and we had our usual bonfire, song time, and prayer circle. It was my favorite part of any youth-group party, but this one was especially great with Duke's head in my lap and Bree all warm on one side of me and now Jake on the other with his big, loose grin. All of us thinking about the same God—except maybe Duke.

"This is all right," I said to Jake.

"Yep. Gottta admit, I kind of like it." He jabbed me in the rib with his elbow. "But next weekend, it's your turn."

"Yeah?" I said vaguely.

"Party at my man Anderson's," Jake went on. "You and Bree gotta come with us."

I looked from Bree to Jake and back again, the way Duke did when he wanted me to throw the ball for him. Both of them looked back at me with suspicion splattered across their faces. Bree got up and moved away.

"We'll talk about it and get back to you," I said, getting up and putting my arm around Bree's shoulder. "She's got a curfew," I said.

"You take Bree home in the truck. Erin and I want to walk," he answered.

I took the key and grabbed Bree's hand. "I'll bring it over to your house in the morning," I said.

He was already walking away from me. "Yep," he said, "and you'll give me an answer about next weekend."

As Jake and Erin jogged off, I turned to Duke who was making it clear that he would like to ride in the back. "Get up front, boy," I said. "Come on." His jaw dropped, but he pulled his haunches out of the sand and hopped up into the front seat.

All the way to Bree's, Duke sat with his back to us, looking longingly out the window. Bree didn't say much either—until we pulled into her driveway. Then she turned right to me.

"When Jake said you had to give him an answer about next weekend," she said, "he was talking about you going to one of his parties, wasn't he?"

I gripped the steering wheel. "Look," I said, "it's not my kind of party either, but I've been thinking about it. We don't have to drink and stuff just because we're there. I mean, aren't we still Christians no matter where we are? Does it matter as long as God is with us?"

She did the stress pull through her hair. "I don't know," she said. "I just don't like it. I won't go with you, Todd. I don't see why you're even considering it."

"Because!" There went my voice, snapping at her again. I grabbed her hand to keep her from yanking it through her hair. "He's gone to every youth-group party I've asked him to. He kind of feels like it's my turn to do something he wants to do for a change. You have to admit, it only sounds fair."

Bree pulled her hand from mind gently and gave me a kiss on the cheek as we pulled into the driveway. "It's late," she said, opening the door. "We'll talk later. Be careful going home." She climbed down and turned to wave as she headed for the house.

As I drove away, Duke lay down on the seat and nuzzled his muzzle into my lap. "This has really got me messed up, Duke," I told him. "I don't want to go to that party. I'm just having a hard time telling Jake why."

Duke sighed softly. I could feel a droplet of drool sinking into my jeans.

"I'm sorry about you not being able to ride in the back," I said. "It's just that you might get hurt. I wouldn't say no if I didn't love you." I sounded like a father.

But something about my last little spiel twanged a string in me. I was coming to a vista point, so I pulled off the road. Duke sprang up, and I opened the window for him. The ocean pounded peacefully in the dark.

"You always get over it, don't you?" I asked.

He didn't answer.

"You pout for a while, but you know I love you. You get over it."

That's what twanged the string. If I said no to Jake, he'd get over it too.

Then it hit me. I'd told Bree I knew she wouldn't be comfortable at the party. I wouldn't push her. Why would I take God there, either, when I knew He wouldn't be comfortable?

That was the "why" I'd been looking for.

"Come on, Duke," I said. "Let's go home."

The scene at Jake's the next morning wasn't a pretty one. He isn't at his best when he has to pry his eyes open at 9:00 A.M. on Saturday and even less so when he pries them open to news he doesn't like. His whole face shriveled into a scowl as I told him I wouldn't go to Anderson's party.

"We can do anything you want to do, guy," I finished up, speaking down into Duke's head as I scratched his ears. "Climb cliffs, run screaming down the beach, carrying the girls piggyback—I don't care—as long as I can feel comfortable asking God to go along with us."

Jake didn't say anything—not even "Yep."

"You're a great friend," I continued, clutching a little at my T-shirt to keep the uneasiness from getting out of control. "I don't want us to stop hanging out. But don't you see where I'm coming from?"

"Nope," he said.

I let go of my T-shirt. "But you'll try?" I asked.

Jake put his hands under his pillow and looked at us both. Duke didn't move his head—only his eyes went from one of us to the other. Slowly the grin crawled across Jake's face. "What am I supposed to do with both of you looking at me like that?" he said.

The relief bubbled out in a chortle. Duke came up pawing and jumped on the bed.

"You're a bud," I said happily.

"Watch and pray so that you will not fall into temptation.
The spirit is willing, but the body is weak."

Matthew 26:41

God Speaks:

You can't avoid temptation, but you can resist it by knowing what is right and sticking to it.

Alone you can't.
Together we can.
—GOD

Just
Like Dad

Everyone's always told me I'm just like my father.

It happened again when my dad's brother, Pete, and his wife were visiting. "Even as a newborn, you had your father's red hair," Uncle Pete said flipping through the photo album.

"And his lungs," Aunt Susan said laughing. "Miranda, could you scream!"

I smiled politely at my aunt and uncle. What I wanted to tell them was that I'd heard all this before, and I didn't want to be like my father in any way, shape, or form.

While Uncle Pete searched the photo album, I fought the urge to grab it from him. *Stop looking at those!* I yelled in my mind. *Stop looking at those pictures of me with the jerk I called Dad for ten years!*

I knew my reaction was overboard, but my dad's red hair wasn't the only thing I'd inherited. I'd gotten his temper too. He used to call me his little spitfire. "Her temper is as red-hot as her hair," he'd tell my mom with pride. "Just like mine."

"Let's hope that changes," Mom always replied.

Unfortunately, it hadn't. My temper is still a problem that God and I wrestle with on a regular basis.

"Miranda," my mom said. "Could you help me?" She could tell my temper was boiling. I was glad to escape.

"What's bothering you?" Mom asked as she shut the kitchen door. "You've been stomping around all morning."

"Melanie was in my stuff again," I snapped. "This morning she had my new sweater. I need my own room and a lock for my closet and drawers!"

"As much as I'd like to give you your own room, I can't. We don't have the space."

"But Melanie is driving me crazy," I wailed. "She gets to do more stuff, go more places, get out of more stupid family get-togethers—"

"Wait a minute," my mom interrupted. "Your sister had already committed to help out at church today."

"So she gets out of an afternoon with Aunt Dull and Uncle Boring, and I'm stuck here," I said. "If I'd known that, I would have volunteered too."

My mom's voice dropped. "Go to your room until you can behave in a way that won't embarrass me in front of our guests."

"Guests! It's just Dad's brother and his wife. He's out of our lives! Why are they still around?"

My mom just pointed to my room. I stomped off. To make sure everyone knew how I felt, I slammed my door. I could hear questions from the living room and my mom reassuring everyone that I was okay.

"I'm not okay!" I screamed through the door. "I'm tired of living in this house and tired of sharing this room!"

The anger I'd kept inside since that morning came pouring out. "I'm done sharing this closet!" I yelled as I yanked my sister's clothes off their hangers and threw them on the floor. If I could have gotten the window open, I would have thrown them outside. If Melanie had been there, I'd have thrown her outside too.

I rearranged my clothes, stepped back, and took a deep breath. "Much better," I announced.

I lay on my bed and began to worry about the consequences of my actions. I knew they wouldn't be far behind.

Yet when my door opened, it was Uncle Pete who walked in.

"Wow," he said stepping over Melanie's clothes. "Is your sister always this messy?"

I didn't even smile. He cleared his throat. "You know, I had a lot of messes like this to clean up in my day. Your dad used to trash our room and then refuse to pick up. 'If you want it clean, you clean it,' he'd say. I hated always running to my mom, so I usually put everything away. It kept the peace."

I looked at Uncle Pete curiously.

"A lot of things in my life didn't seem fair," he went on. "Sharing a room with my brother—" I nodded, "and my dad walking out were two of the biggest."

"So how'd you get through it?" I asked.

Uncle Pete looked at me closely. "By depending on the same two people you probably depend on in your life—my mom and God."

I nodded.

"Miranda, I know you're angry about how life's treated you, but you have to realize you're not the only one affected by your temper. Your mom and sister are too."

"But I can't change," I said, thinking of all the times God and I had wrestled with it. "When I'm angry, it's like I'm out of control."

"That's okay. As long as you give God the control you've lost."

I wondered what Uncle Pete meant.

"Your dad used to tell me he couldn't control his temper. What he meant was that he couldn't control it without God's help. He has finally accepted that fact in the last couple years, and he's letting God help him do what he couldn't do on his own."

I was amazed that my dad had turned to God. Uncle Pete's news gave me a flicker of hope.

My uncle smiled. "I came in to apologize for upsetting you with those pictures. When I got them out, I was trying to remember the good times, not remind you of things you'd rather forget."

"It's okay," I told him. "I need to concentrate on the good times too."

"You got a lot of positive qualities from your dad, too, you know," Uncle Pete said as he got up to leave. "His sense of humor, his willingness to work hard, his determination—don't forget those things."

I surveyed the mess I made and laughed. "It's a good thing I got my dad's willingness to work hard."

Uncle Pete grinned as he shut the door.

As I picked up Melanie's clothes, I thought about what Uncle Pete had said. "God, I know I'm stuck with the red hair," I prayed, "but I'm determined to work on my temper just like my dad."

I can do all things through Christ who strengthens me.

Philippians 4:13 NKJV

God Speaks:

With My help, you can overcome any weakness and become all that I have created you to be.

Just where is this
relationship going,
anyway?
—GOD

Keep in Touch

shley reached for the big picture of Eric on her bedside table. As she did every night, she pressed her lips lightly to the glass covering his mouth and whispered, "Good night, Eric."

She snuggled under the covers, thinking about Eric, who was a freshman at a college in California. "A picture's not much to have, but he writes every other day. And calls me once a week. That's the best thing—hearing his voice. I wish he weren't so far away!"

She took a deep breath and closed her eyes. "God, please be with Eric and with all your people everywhere." She breathed a soft "Amen" and rolled into her favorite sleeping position.

When the alarm went off, Ashley fumbled for the off button, sat up, and looked at Eric's picture. "Good morning." She kissed the glass again. "Have a good day, and don't forget me! I'll be thinking of you all day."

She dressed quickly and reread Eric's last letter. It was so funny. Ashley could almost hear his voice. She returned the letter to the nightstand.

Later at her locker, Ashley smiled at the picture of Eric and her pasted on the inside of the door. It was his last day at home before leaving for college, and they were both smiling as they held hands.

"Hi, Ashley. Still weak over that picture, I see."

Ashley spun around as Shelley, her best friend and pastor's daughter, approached.

"It's the last one I have of him!" Ashley defended. "It reminds me of what we said to each other that last day. We promised to keep in touch, so nothing would come between us."

Shelley nodded. "I know. You're always talking about Eric!"

"Are you saying I should forget him because he's in college now, and I'm still in high school?"

"I don't think you should forget him," Shelley said slowly. "I just think you shouldn't let him take up your whole life! You didn't come to youth group last week because Eric was going to call. I know he didn't know we changed the night, but he would have called back. And you didn't want to help paint the children's room at church because you had to write to Eric that night. And you said you didn't think you'd be at the Bible study my dad's starting tonight. It just seems like Eric's your whole life!"

"You're starting to talk like my parents! Or like yours!"

"Being a pastor's daughter doesn't make me different!" Shelley snapped.

"I know. I'm sorry. But how can you say Eric's taking over my life! You know we promised each other we'd keep in touch."

"OK, I'm sorry too," Shelley said. "You're my best friend, but somehow, lately, nothing seems to count with you but Eric. Not even God!"

The warning bell cut off their talk. Ashley hurried one way while Shelley rushed the other.

Ashley tried to forget the conversation. At noon, she carried her tray through the noisy cafeteria to the table where her friends always sat. Everyone was eating except Debbie, who sat staring at her plate.

"My brother called last night from training camp," Debbie said. "He and his girlfriend broke up. They just drifted apart, he said because they were so far away from each other. I'm taking it harder than he is. I really liked her."

Ashley glanced at Shelley. She knew what her friend was thinking, but she was wrong! "That can't happen to Eric and me! We're keeping in touch! We write every other day, and he calls me a lot too."

"But that doesn't always work." Another girl had stopped eating. "My sister wrote every day to her boyfriend when he was an exchange student in Brazil. Sent him pictures and stuff to eat. But they broke up when he got back. You never can tell."

"You got that right!" someone else put in. "My cousin and her boyfriend—"

Now everyone was talking about couples who had broken up. Everyone seemed to know of at least one example. Ashley tried not to listen to the stories. She told herself they were about other people; they didn't have anything to do with Eric and her. It would never happen to them if they worked at keeping in touch regularly. If they did that, they'd be okay.

By the end of the day Ashley was convinced that she and Eric were different. She met Shelley at their locker, feeling confident again.

"You think anymore about coming to Bible study tonight?" Shelley asked, pulling books from the shelf. "I don't think there'll be many there—only those who want to keep in touch with God."

"I don't know," Ashley said. "I have a lot of homework, and this is my night to write to Eric. I have a lot to tell him."

"Think about it. Maybe you can get your homework done before dinner and write Eric after Bible study. It's only going to be an hour."

"Maybe." Ashley grabbed her books and ran to the bus, hoping it would go quickly so she could see if she had received a letter from Eric.

In the house, Ashley swallowed her disappointment when there was no letter waiting for her. *I should call Shelley right now and tell her I'm skipping Bible study. I have to write to Eric tonight; I don't want to lose touch with him!*

She went to her room, but as she reached for paper to start her letter to Eric, she noticed her Bible. Suddenly Shelley's words about the Bible study came back to her. *Only those who want to keep in touch with God.*

I promised to keep in touch with Eric, Ashley thought, *and I've been trying hard to do that. But I promised to stay close to God, too, and I haven't done much about that lately. I haven't talked to Him—not really talked—or read what He wrote to me. I haven't even thought about Him all day!*

She paused and picked up Eric's picture. "I guess we could break up—people do, and we're too young to talk about marriage anyway. If we broke up, we'd both get over it eventually, but if I broke up with God—"

Ashley picked up her Bible. *I'll call Shelley and tell her to save me a seat tonight,* she thought. *Afterwards, I'll write Eric all about it and why I'm going! He'll understand!*

Now, dear children, continue in him, so that when he appears we may be confident and unashamed before him at his coming.

1 John 2:28

God Speaks:

To nurture your relationship with Me, you must make a commitment of time, energy, and attention.

Do I have an offer
for you!

—GOD

Legal Wall

" Scottie! Cop, dude!"

"No way, man!"

"I see his light! Come on—let's go!"

I swore and dropped the spray can. It was still half full, and who knew when I'd have the chance to rack another one. Worse, the wall wasn't done.

"Let's go, dude! I can hear him!"

I crouched low to get to the fence, my mouth already going dry. Brent was at the top of the chain link, and Darryl scrambled up it like a monkey. From inside the warehouse, somebody was shining a big flashlight, and the beam swept right over the top of Darryl's head. I curled my fingers into the fence and then stopped.

"Man—I gotta go back," I hissed.

"You'll get caught!"

But I headed back toward the warehouse wall anyway. The can I'd thrown away had my fat tip on it, my only one. I got down on my hands and knees and crawled over the gravel. My hand came down on the can at the same instant the light shot right into my eyes.

"All right, Picasso, get up nice and slow."

It didn't register at first that it was a woman's voice. All I could think about were the stories I'd heard about what cop-wanna-be security guards did to "taggers" as they called us. I didn't get up, slow or otherwise; I just stayed there and tried to think how to get away before he—she—could grab me.

I cupped my hand around the can and found the sprayer with my finger. In one smooth move, I sprang up and aimed the can at her face. In an even smoother one, she knocked the can out of my hand with her nightstick and had the stick poised to knock my head off. I froze.

So did she.

"Ms. Kirkendoll!" I exclaimed.

She ran the flashlight up and down me. "Scottie Byrd."

She swept the light over the wall I'd been working on, but I didn't run. What would be the point? She was my art teacher.

"Doing a little homework, I see," she said dryly.

"Doing a little moonlighting, I see," I said, nodding at the uniform.

"I do it for the extra money," she said. "What's your excuse?"

I shrugged. "Why don't you just haul me in?"

"And have people find out one of my art students did that piece of trash?"

"It wouldn't be trash if I had had time to perfect it!" I said. "I'm no toy."

"Toy?"

"Some sorry artist who just writes out of disrespect," I said.

"This isn't disrespect? You probably know the consequences if I call the police," she said. "A thousand bucks. Probation officer dogging your trail for a year. I'd start talking if I were you."

"If I can convince you I had a reason for doing this, you won't turn me in?"

"Try me," she said.

"I write," I said, "so I can become known. I want fame. Respect."

"I'm not following."

"Okay—I'm developing my own style, see—it's wild—I take a word or a figure, and I twist it, so it's like nobody else's. Then I get it up all over town—cover whole walls with my pieces—and I get known. People respect me."

"I can see that," she said finally. "But this is somebody's property."

"A blank wall is an open invitation," I said.

"Oh—and so is my house, my car—"

"No, man, I don't do private property or bomb schools, either."

"What's a bomb?"

"That's when you just got time to come in and write one quick thing." I pointed to what I'd done. "Like I did my name."

"Zooloo," she read.

"That's the name I gave myself—it's what started the whole hip-hop culture—the Zooloo tribes—"

She stopped me with her flashlight. "It's still illegal."

"If we had legal walls to do pieces on, we wouldn't hit this kind of stuff," I said.

"I find that hard to believe."

"Who cares? You'll never find out because nobody's ever going to give us that chance."

She stuck her nightstick back in its holder and put her hands on her hips.

"Back that up, Zooloo," she said. "Come into the art room tomorrow morning, one hour before school starts."

She shot me one more time with the flashlight and headed back to the warehouse. It was a full minute before I booked over the fence. And it was a full night before I decided whether or not I was going to show up. But I was standing at the art-room door when she got there. I wasn't anxious to go to jail.

She pointed sleepily at a bare wall at the end of the room and said, "Go for it. Do your perfect piece," she said. "There's a legal wall."

I stared at her.

"Look, Zooloo," she said irritably, "don't make me explain it, okay? I'm not a morning person. You're lucky I've said this much. I want the whole wall covered by the end of the week. There are supplies in those cabinets," and she shuffled out.

If we had legal walls to do pieces on, I'd told her, *we wouldn't hit public property.*

Well, there it was. I could take my time and perfect a piece. I could actually do my art right there, and it would all be legal. And suddenly it didn't sound like that much fun.

She had not done a thing to me except give me a chance, and I hated her just as much as I hated every other adult that crossed my path, no matter what they did. I knew in that flash of a second that it wasn't about fame or respect or the hip-hop culture at all. It was about expressing hate, and I was using the thing I loved best to do it. My art.

I opened a cabinet and stared, unseeing, at the paint. The only thing I could see was the crossroads I was standing at. Take the chance and prove I was an artist—or prove I was nothing but a toy. A lying, stealing, running toy.

That was Tuesday. Wednesday, Darryl and Brent sauntered in.

"Why are you kissing up?" Darryl asked.

"We always said we wanted a legal wall. She gave me one, that's all."

"Yeah, but what's the catch? There's gotta be a catch."

"Fellow graffiti artists, Zooloo?" Ms. Kirkendoll asked as she walked through the door.

"You gentlemen feel free to grab a paint brush," she said. "I can clear off another wall."

Darryl grunted, and Ms. K. went back in the supply room. Darryl put his mouth close to my ear. "The crew says doing this is like you're dissin' them," he said.

"I just want to do my art," I said.

"Then you don't want to hang with us."

He jerked his head toward the door. Brent cast one more admiring look at my wall and then followed Darryl. Everything I'd had to give me an identity had just walked out.

I looked down at the paint brush I was holding and dipped it into a can of red. One more section before class.

By Friday I was done. Ms. Kirkendoll was already examining the wall and frowning when I got there.

"Something's missing," she said.

I felt strangely disappointed. I guess I'd kind of wanted her to like it.

"What?" I asked.

"Your name. How will you get fame unless you put 'Zooloo' on there?"

I shrugged. "I guess I didn't do it for fame."

"Really?" she said. "I thought that was what this was all about—getting known, getting respect."

I shrugged again and started to back away.

"It's a beautiful piece, Scottie. It says a lot about you."

"I was just writing about art," I said, "the way I see it."

"It's the same thing. Your art is you."

"Can I ask you a question?" I asked.

"Sure," she said.

"Why did you do this—you know, give me a chance? Were you trying to prove something to me?"

She smiled. "I did it because God put every human being here with a chance. It's my job to be sure every kid of mine gets that chance. Whether you take it or not is up to you, of course."

I looked her square in the eye. "Be honest," I said. "Did you think I'd take the chance?"

She didn't flinch. "Have you?" she asked.

It's a question I've been asking myself ever since. Am I just ticked off, or am I trying to express a creative side of me that needs to come out? I ask myself that every time I pass the spray-paint display in the hardware store. Every time I drive by a blank wall under a freeway. Every time I break out the paint in the art room and start putting myself up on yet another legal wall.

"I know the plans I have for you," declares the LORD, "plans to prosper you and not to harm you, plans to give you hope and a future."

Jeremiah 29:11

God Speaks:

When you have a relationship with Me, I promise to love, encourage, and shape you into exactly who you were meant to be.

Have you read my
#1 best-seller.
(There will be a test.)
—GOD

Lessons from Summer School

I should have known something was up the moment Mr. Day walked into our English class. He lugged in a briefcase big enough to carry all fifteen volumes of *Encyclopedia Britannica.* Instead, it held the many costumes he would use for our class. He also wore a smile that said, "You won't believe what I have in store for you this summer!"

"Ladies and gentlemen," he announced, "it's my privilege to teach this summer session of English Literature. I realize some of you are here because you want to be and others because you need to be. Either way, I think you'll enjoy this class!"

He waited as if expecting us to break out in wild applause. We didn't.

Undaunted, Mr. Day passed out books and launched right into the first class.

As I surveyed the room, I saw some nerdy brainiacs and a couple kids who'd failed the class and needed to take it over to move on—like me.

I'd seen the words "summer school" looming in my future since January. By then, my parents' divorce had been final for a couple months. I'd told myself it was no big deal, but my grades told another story.

"Are you sure everything's okay?" my mom asked as she looked through the grade slips. "Do you want to talk? Maybe if you go to church with me this week—"

I gave her a look that told her I wasn't interested—not in talking, not in church, not in God. While she'd "found religion" after Dad left, I didn't want any part of it. Sure God and I had had quite a few loud and angry conversations right after the divorce, but He wasn't part of my life. God and I got together two times a year—Christmas and Easter. I even went to church for the celebrations. It felt like it was enough—for me—but apparently it wasn't for my mom.

Whenever something bothered me, she'd ask again if I wanted to go with her on Sunday. "How can you know God doesn't fit into your life if you don't even know Him?" she'd asked me. I didn't have an answer.

But the answer to my less-than-stellar grade slips meant sitting in a classroom for four weeks with a man who delighted in dressing up as characters from the books we read. It would, he said, help us get to know them. And, he added, knowing the characters is the first step to understanding what the story is all about.

So Mr. Day became Hamlet, Sherlock Holmes, Heathcliff, Mr. Rochester, and a number of other equally memorable characters. As we worked through the books, he drilled us with questions: "What is the character feeling right now?" "Why did the character act that way?" "With whom do you identify in this story?"

He was right. Between his costumed performances and penetrating questions, I was getting to know the people who populated the great stories of English literature. I understood

Heathcliff's brooding nature and sympathized with Jane Eyre's feelings of abandonment.

Sometimes when I was reading, I'd hear Mr. Day's questions echoing in my mind in a different way. *What am I feeling right now? Why am I acting this way? Who do I identify with?* I didn't have answers for those questions. My parents' divorce had left me wondering who I was.

One night, my search led me to Mom's room where I grabbed her Bible. It took awhile to find the book of John, but I finally did. Mom had always said that when I was ready for God, it would be a good place to start. I wasn't sure I was ready, but I did want to know if He had any answers for me.

I started reading about the Word being from the beginning and being with God—about all things being made through Him . . . about the light in Him being life, and the darkness not under-standing it.

I snapped the book shut. I don't understand it either! I thought. *I'm not going to find any answers here!*

The next day at school, I stayed after class to talk to Mr. Day. "What happens when you come up against a book you don't understand?" I asked.

Mr. Day stopped putting his papers away. "Have you gotten to know the characters?"

"Not as well as I should," I confessed.

"How much have you read?"

I squirmed.

"And you're wondering why you don't understand this book?" he snorted. "What's giving you so much difficulty?"

I paused. "The Bible."

Mr. Day's eyes softened. "Ah," he said, as if that explained everything. "Are you reading it as literature or for relationship?"

I looked at him, perplexed.

"For you, is the Bible a bunch of stories or is it what gives your life meaning?"

"That's what I'm trying to find out," I told him. "I started reading, but I didn't understand it."

"Sometimes," Mr. Day said, "you have to read beyond the words."

"How do I do that?"

"You must figure that out yourself," he said with a smile.

So that night I went back to the Bible. As I did, Mr. Day's words came back to me, "Knowing the characters is the first step to understanding what the story is all about."

So instead of turning to the book of John, I looked for the words in red—Jesus' words. *Tell me about Yourself,* I thought. As I read, I learned that the greatest person is the one who is the servant of all. That to find your life you have to give it away. That to really live, you must be born again.

I read the words over and over.

All my life, the only praying I'd done had been those desperate hour-of-need missiles shot heavenward in a last-minute attempt to earn a good grade on a test. I wanted this prayer to be different. Life without God was empty, and I didn't want it to be empty anymore.

"God, it's me," I started.

Your word is a lamp to my feet and a light for my path.

Psalm 119:105

God Speaks:

The Bible isn't just a book; it's a letter from Me, explaining who I am, who you are, and how the two of us can get to know each other better.

> **Live for me; I died for you.**
>
> **—GOD**

Man's Best Friend

It was the day before Thanksgiving, and I knew I should be thankful—for getting over the flu, for inheriting Mom's ancient Chevy, even for Mom's "We'll see about going to church tomorrow."

Twisting my key in the lock, I pushed open the front door. At least Dad would be home for Thanksgiving. Mom was probably picking him up at the airport right then. The answering machine light flashed in the silence, so I punched the play button.

"Teddy," Mom's voice crackled from her car phone, "there's leftover pot roast in the frig—" Her voice faded. "—the trash cans up—." The machine clicked off.

"Trash cans," I muttered, feeling the loneliness sink in. Heading back outside, I heard Mrs. McGregor's cockapoos yipping, and I waved.

She peered at me over her glasses. "That's the sorriest excuse for a smile—"

I sighed. "I'm okay, Mrs. McGregor. It's just, Dad's been working in Washington, and Mom went to pick him up at the airport."

Mrs. McGregor's face puckered into a frown. "It's not healthy to eat alone. Thank goodness I have Annabelle and Melinda." She glanced at her dogs then smiled. "That's what you need— a dog."

"A dog?" I'd love one, but I knew what Mom would say.

"Teddy, be practical."

Dad would add, "In a few years, you'll be going to college. What will we do with a dog when you're gone?"

I shrugged. "A dog sounds great, Mrs. McGregor, but—" I explained about my parents.

"Well, now," she murmured, trying to unwind her dogs' leashes. "My niece told me about a guide-dog program. People raise puppies for a year. Then you give the dogs back, and they're trained to be guide dogs."

"A dog for a year?" It sounded perfect. The question was, would Mom and Dad agree? "Please, God," I whispered. I'd prayed about being lonely before, prayed about Mom and Dad, prayed about a lot of things. But nothing ever changed, and sometimes I wondered if God really cared. Maybe this time.

I waited until morning to mention it to Mom and Dad. Mom sighed. "Teddy, be practical." Before Dad could start, I explained about the guide-dog program.

"You have to give the dog back?" Dad asked, one eyebrow raised.

I nodded. "After a year." My parents exchanged a look, then a quick nod.

Thank you, God, I whispered in my heart.

The week before Christmas, I brought home a Labrador puppy named Wallis. Mom ruffled her yellow fur. "Wallis's doghouse can be your Christmas present."

"No doghouse." I tossed a tennis ball for Wallis to chase. "She sleeps with me."

"Sleeps with you?"

"In my room anyway. When she's a guide dog, her master might need her at night." Wallis galloped back with the soggy ball. I rubbed my face in her fur.

Usually I felt crummy going to church by myself, especially on Christmas Eve. But this time, Wallis was with me.

Before we left, I slipped the blue cape on her back. The bright yellow letters read,

"Puppy in Training." Wallis rolled over and tried to rub the pack off. "No, Wallis," I murmured, scratching her chest. She relaxed under my hand. "The cape is for practice, like the harness you'll wear when you're working."

Sitting up, she tipped her head sideways. "Trust me," I whispered, leaning over so she could nuzzle my neck.

The snow had started that afternoon. By the time I parked at church, there were a couple of inches on the ground.

"Hey, Ted! Catch!" A snowball flew toward me. Dodging, I swiped up a handful of snow and flung it back at my friend.

"Woof!" Wallis leapt into the air, snapping at the snow.

"No, Wallis, sit," I ordered. Whining, she looked up at me like the only kid at recess with a time out. "Regular dogs can play," I whispered, kneeling to put my arms around her neck. "You're special. You have an important job to do." Pushing to my feet, I waved at Andy. "Sorry, we can't play." I explained about the guide-dog program.

"Cool." Andy fell into step beside us, then pulled open the church door.

The usher gave me an apologetic smile. "I'm sorry, Ted, but you can't bring your dog in here."

Andy grinned. "It's okay, Mr. Morris. She's a guide dog."

The usher frowned at me. "But you're not blind."

"I'm helping train her for someone who is. She goes with me everywhere, so she gets used to being around people." Wallis sat quietly at my side, the perfect lady.

Mr. Morris patted my shoulder. "That's terrific, Ted. You go on in."

I slipped into the back row, and Wallis sat close to my feet. I felt the warmth of her body against my leg as I started to sing, "O little town of Bethlehem, how still we see thee lie."

Wallis lifted her head for a moment, then settled back down, her chin on my shoe. I was glad they didn't ask us to stand. She seemed so content.

Actually, having to take Wallis everywhere turned out to be great. She waited in line with me at the post office. She sat beside me at basketball games. She even stayed awake while I crammed for my chemistry final.

I'd been nervous about taking her to the grocery store, but by summer I decided she was ready. All I needed was bread and lettuce. But as we walked into Food Mart, the manager stopped us.

"You can't bring a dog in here."

Smiling, I started to explain about the guide-dog program.

"No dogs in the grocery store. You can't expect a dog to just walk past the meat aisle."

"But she will," I promised. "If she can't, they won't let her be a guide dog."

"One chance," he told me quietly. "The first complaint I get, she waits outside."

I swallowed hard, then nodded. With a quick tug on her leash, I started into the store. The bread aisle was first, and I grabbed the first loaf I saw. Wallis was looking around, but so far, she seemed content at my side.

"Good girl," I whispered, leaning down to stroke her head. I'd been keeping my eye on a little girl swinging her legs in a cart across the aisle. Suddenly, the cookie she was gnawing dropped to the floor. Wallis padded forward, sniffing—

"No, Wallis."

"Doggie!" squealed the girl.

"Dog?" Her mother looked startled. "Where?"

"Cookie!" cried the girl as Wallis's pink tongue wiped over the treat.

"Oh, no." I tugged Wallis's collar. "Sit!" Obediently, Wallis settled down on her back legs, but it was too late to save the cookie. "I'm really sorry—"

The mother smiled. "I wouldn't have let my daughter eat if off the floor anyway." Digging into her purse, she pulled out a bag with another cookie. "A future guide dog, huh. One of my Girl Scouts was telling me about that."

"It's really neat," I agreed nervously. "I—I think I'd better get going. She's still new at this."

"Of course." The mother scooped up the cookie and held it toward Wallis. "She might as well—"

"No, Wallis!" This time she stayed beside me, and I patted her head. "She really can't," I explained. "If I let her do it sometimes, she won't know when it's not okay."

The mother chuckled. "It works about the same way with children."

Waving good-bye to the little girl, I decided to skip the lettuce. Wallis had learned enough for one day.

By fall Wallis and I were doing all the grocery shopping. She seemed to like football as much as basketball, but I felt like a shadow was hovering over us. Our one-year anniversary was getting closer every day.

I was home alone the night the phone rang. "Wallis won't start her formal training until January," the lady at the foundation told me, "but she'll need to get used to our facilities. Could you bring her back next week?"

That was the longest week of my life. I prayed that God would let me keep Wallis, or make me feel better, or do something to stop the pain. Nothing happened, and I wondered if Wallis was the only one in the world who listened to me, who loved me. How could I give her up?

That was the question I asked all the way to the foundation. The lady there must have understood because she took us to a large building with a street reconstructed inside. We watched a blind man guided by another Labrador walk around an open gate, avoid a skateboard, and edge past some low branches.

Beside me, Wallis sat at attention. She seemed to know something special was happening, and despite all the pain inside, I knew it too.

I didn't say goodbye. I just bent down and scratched her head, then handed her leash to the lady. But that night, lying in the darkness, I cried.

Somehow I got through the last two days of school. Dad was working in town for a change, and he and Mom bought a tree, but it didn't seem to matter to me. In fact, I almost didn't go to church on Christmas Eve. But staying home and thinking about Wallis was worse, so I slipped in and sat in the back.

The little kids were acting out the manger scene. Then the minister stepped forward. "For God so loved the world, that He gave His only begotten Son—"

I didn't hear the rest. All I could think about was how much I loved Wallis and how much it had hurt to give her up, even to a loving home. Could I have done it, if I'd known she was going to be killed?

Around me, people were standing as the organ started playing "Joy to the World." But I sat still, letting the realization sink in. If you believed God gave His Son to die for your sins, you had to believe in God's love, no matter what was happening in your life. If God didn't love us, He never could have done it.

All the voices around me started singing. I stood and joined in. "Joy to the world, the Lord is come!"

"God so loved the world that he gave his one and only Son, that whoever believes in him shall not perish but have eternal life."

John 3:16

God Speaks:

Would you give up something you really value for the sake of others?

Will the road you're on
take you to my place?
—GOD

Measure Off the Original

I hate school. Well, that's not entirely true. Shop isn't bad. I'm one of two girls in the class—just Beth, me, and twenty-seven boys. Instead of Lori, the guys call me Miss Goodwrench, but that's okay. I'm kind of a tomboy.

In fact, what I really want is to be a great tennis player. And I've got a good start. I'm the first freshman to make Fairview High's varsity team. But as of 2:45 yesterday, the next step toward great looked like it would take longer than I thought.

It started yesterday morning at my locker.

"Lori! Lori, wait!"

The hall was crowded, but I saw the tennis coach and waved.

"Lori, I've got a terrific surprise." Coach Carver grinned. "The doctor told Cathy to stay off her ankle for a week, so tomorrow you'll be playing doubles."

Singles and doubles? My skin prickled all over. *Venus Williams, watch out!*

"You'll have to practice a couple of hours after dinner, though," the coach warned.

Half my prickles faded. "But—"

"No buts, kiddo. You and Brenda need to get used to playing together."

Nodding, I ran toward my English class. Every last prickle had vanished. All that was left was a large cold lump in my stomach. I couldn't practice after dinner. I had a history paper due the next day—five pages on the Peloponnesian War.

After English, I ran a fast detour through the new wing and stopped at my history room. "Mr. Ellis?" I gulped air, waiting for him to nod. He looked like a history teacher. I'd never seen him without his dark suit and white shirt, and he said he had one gray hair for every student he'd taught.

With a sharp nod, he told me to go ahead.

"Can I have an extra day to finish my history report?" I blurted out. "I have this emergency tennis practice—"

"No."

"But—"

"You know the rules, Lori. No reports accepted late. Period."

"But Mr.—"

"You'll have to decide what your priorities are."

I sighed dramatically, but I'd known it was hopeless. I spent the rest of the morning trying to think of a way out. But it kept coming down to one thing: I couldn't be in two places at once. I had to choose between an F on my paper and giving up my chance to play doubles.

And then, as I was logging onto the Internet in the computer lab, I discovered there was another choice.

A banner ad scrolled across the screen: "TERM PAPERS: MORE THAN 20,000 SUBJECTS ON FILE—FREE!"

I swallowed. Would the Peloponnesian War be in the top twenty thousand subjects?

I didn't click on the ad. I knew it was wrong. There wasn't a lot of difference between copying someone's test and downloading a term paper.

"Hey, Lori."

I glanced back and saw Cathy leaning on her crutches. "How you doing?"

She rolled her eyes. "You'd think my ankle was broken the way my mom carried on. But if I have to be out, I'm so glad you're the one subbing for me." She hobbled over and whispered, "Brenda's backhand isn't too good, so you'll have to poach a little when you're in the left court."

I was nodding when I remembered my paper. "I don't know if I'll be able to play."

"What are you talking about?" Cathy demanded.

"Shhhhh!" the lab supervisor hissed.

Cathy leaned closer and whispered, "This is your big chance to get some experience. After playing singles and doubles for a couple of weeks with Brenda, making the doubles team next fall will be a no-brainer. Maybe we can even play together."

I sighed. She was right.

"Ladies!"

Cathy waved at the supervisor with her crutch and headed toward an empty seat at the end of the row. I rolled my mouse around, watching the cursor race around the screen. Finally I clicked on the banner ad. It wasn't a crime to check, and they probably didn't have the Peloponnesian War anyway.

They did.

You know that voice in the back of your head that bugs you when you're watching this great movie on TV but you're supposed to be washing the dishes? Well, it started talking to me.

What will your friends think?

They won't find out, I snapped back.

But what would they think if they knew?

Nothing! And it's not like they were better than I. Last week Amanda's mom hemmed the skirt for her Home-Ec project. And when our youth group was baby-sitting the toddlers, Danny pretended he'd never had measles, so he wouldn't have to help. So why couldn't I download a history paper?

The paper was in my notebook when I walked into my shop class. We were making flower planters. Mr. Hubert put on his safety goggles and lined up his pieces of wood.

"The pieces must be identical," he warned. "I-den-ti-cal." He glared at the circle of students through his goggles. "Fifteen inches long and a quarter-inch hole one inch from each end. Measure the first one with a ruler." He made two pencil marks and drilled the holes. "Use your first board as a pattern." He marked another board and drilled it.

"Use—" Rapping on the counter with his ruler, he waited until the room was quiet. "Use the original board as the pattern for all the others. Is that clear?"

"Why?" The thin voice came from in front of Mr. Hubert. Arthur. I groaned. No one except Arthur ever cared why.

Mr. Hubert smiled. He likes Arthur. "No matter how careful you are, your holes may be off. Your drill could slip, maybe just an eighth of an inch. If you use the second board to mark the third and you're off again, the third board will be a quarter of an inch off. Each time you use a different board, you compound the error, and by the time you've cut all sixteen boards, you could be two inches off, even though you only made a tiny mistake.

The class nodded. We always nod. It's easier.

Mr. Hubert slapped his ruler on the desk. "Get started."

Around me, I heard the other kids moving, getting their lumber, finding drill bits. But I was thinking.

God is like the original board. He's exactly right. And I should pattern my life after His. If I try to live like other people, even other Christians, it's like using the second or third board. I'll be copying their mistakes, getting further and further from God.

My planter didn't look great. My mind was on other things, like Amanda's mom hemming her skirt and Danny lying about having the measles. But God didn't cheat or lie, for any reason, and He was the One I needed to measure my life by.

So when the final bell rang at 2:45, I threw away the paper on the Peloponnesian War and told Coach Carver I couldn't make the extra practice. She wasn't very happy with my decision, but I felt like God was, and His approval meant even more than playing tennis.

Teach me your way, O Lord, and I will walk in your truth.

Psalm 86:11

God Speaks:

I've given you the right to choose; choose to do what is right.

My Brother, My Friend

Ever since I could remember, my brother, Michael, and I had been fighting—over stuff like who had a bigger piece of cake or who got to ride in the front seat on a three-block ride to the grocery store.

But when I started high school, two years behind Michael, things changed. It started when I brought home my class schedule the first day. He was in the kitchen foraging, and I went in to catch any crumbs that might be left over.

"Who do you have for geometry?" he asked.

I looked around the kitchen. "Who—me?"

"I don't see anybody else in here."

"Cranston," I said.

"No way! Get out of that class—he's a slave driver."

"But I can't get a schedule change now! They said—"

"Forget they. I got connections. Who've you got for English?"

Later it hit me that we'd gotten though an entire conversation without snarling. I didn't even slam my door when I went to my room. I'd have figured he'd just mistaken me for some stranger passing through the kitchen, except that wasn't the end of it.

The next week he got his license, and naturally he looked for excuses to drive. Mom caught on fast and started having him cart me to gymnastics and choir practice.

During those rides, he'd coach me on how to get through Getz's essay tests, and we started calling each other Bro and Sis instead of Pizza Face and Miss Piggy. I wouldn't say we were "close," but I was at least convinced that if my skin accidentally touched his, he wasn't going to run for the cootie-killing spray.

On Michael's first weekend night to take the car out, he was supposed to be in by 11:00. At 11:15 he called.

"Flat tire," Dad said when he hung up the phone. "Oldest excuse in the book. Does he think we're stupid?"

"I think 'lame' is the word they use now," Mom said.

It occurred to me that maybe Michael *had* had a flat tire. It didn't occur to our parents until he came home and showed them the spare on the right rear.

"Oh, okay," Dad said. "Let's get to bed."

Michael was the first one to go, slamming his door behind him.

When around midnight I heard him come out of his room, I followed him to the kitchen.

"He could have at least apologized for not believing you," I said, handing him the peanut butter he couldn't locate because males can never move anything to find what they want.

"No doubt. It's like they raise this son—and then look for reasons not to trust him. Why is there never anything to eat in this house?"

"There's cold pizza in the meat drawer."

"How come you always know this stuff?"

"I'm female."

He looked at me as if he'd never considered that before. Then he plopped a plate of Mom's homemade pizza on the table and scraped the chair up to it.

"Want some?" he asked.

We ate and talked—about everything—what it was like being raised by Mom and Dad, what we liked and didn't like about school. We even told each other how we pray.

"You know what's cool?" he asked.

"What?"

"We used to hate each other. Now we actually pray to the same God."

I couldn't sleep that night until I finally put something together. If you share the most secret part of yourself with a friend, you get a little nagging doubt later because you're afraid they might tell somebody else. But when your friend is your brother, you don't have that because he's family.

Or so I thought.

That Tuesday after school, I went into the kitchen to empty the dishwasher and found Michael in there with two of his basketball buddies, Jason and Scott. They were sitting at the kitchen table, practically salivating, and Michael was pulling open drawers and slamming cabinet doors.

"Do you have a search warrant?" I asked.

"I smell brownies—I know Mom made brownies."

"Mom and Dad are gone until after dinner," I said. "She made us a casserole and brownies."

"Where are they?"

I lifted the lid to the cookie jar.

"Thanks, Miss P.," he said and pinched my cheek.

I stared at him as he tucked the cookie jar under his arm and plopped down at the table with it.

"We got any milk?" he asked, his mouth crammed.

"Try the refrigerator," I said.

I turned my back and started yanking glasses out of the dishwasher.

"Michael says you're a freshman," Jason said.

"Unfortunately," I said.

"You don't look it."

"Give her time, man. She'll catch up," Michael said. "She hasn't lost all her baby fat yet."

Before I could hurl a stack of plates at him, Jason said, "No—I mean, you look older than that. I saw you working out with the J.V. girls' basketball team the other day, and I went 'Whoa, what's the junior doing on J.V.?'"

Michael proceeded to choke on a brownie and lunge for his milk glass.

"You oughta come shoot some baskets with us," Jason said to me.

Michael made a miraculous recovery and yelled, "No way!" Then he held out his empty glass to me. "Why don't you put this in the dishwasher before you run on along, huh?"

I didn't "run on along." I smiled sweetly at them all, except for Michael at whom I curled my upper lip, and then I swept from the kitchen, cookie jar in hand.

By the time I got to my room—and slammed the door—every inch of me was stinging. I'd played Michael's game and maybe even won, but the fact that he'd even started it cut me to the bone.

So much for our 'friendship,' Brother. You make me look like a fool in front of your friends, just when I think I can trust you to treat me like a person. I hate you! I thought—and then stopped.

The thing was that I didn't hate him. We had a real relationship now, only he was playing around with it like it was a stupid basketball.

I pulled a brownie out of the cookie jar, but before I could stuff it in my mouth, I stopped. What about me? What about the sweet exit I'd just made from the kitchen? And was I now going to sit around and wait for him to make the next move?

I wasn't sure yet.

Around 6:00, I heard Michael alone in the kitchen. He must have opened and closed the refrigerator door five times.

My mind was saying, "I hope you starve," but my feet took me out there, where I opened the door to the fridge, moved the milk carton, found the casserole, and popped it into the microwave. I was moving like a robot, and Michael wasn't much looser. He stood in the middle of the kitchen and mumbled, "Will we need ketchup for that?"

"I would assume so," I said icily, "since you put ketchup on everything."

With no attempt to locate the bottle, he barked, "Where is it?"

I turned around and plastered myself against the pantry door. "It's in here," I said. "But you're not getting it until you answer a question for me—honestly."

Michael rolled his eyes.

"Why would you start a really good friendship with somebody—and then turn around and make them look stupid in front of people?"

"I would never do that!" Michael said. "Ask any of my friends!"

I leaped across the room to face my reflection in the microwave door. "Mandy," I said to it. "I thought you were one of Michael's friends. Has he ever done that to you?" I put both hands up to my face. "Why, yes, as a matter of fact. Just today he made a total fool out of me in front of two guys because he doesn't want them to know we're friends! Not his little sister!"

"Oh, come on, Mandy!" Michael said. "It's a whole different—"

I spun around to face him. "If we're going to be friends, then it has to be all the time, not just when nobody else is looking."

The microwave dinged, and I flung it open. "Stir it and put it in for three more minutes on high," I said as I headed for the door. "I'm not hungry anymore."

"Hey—" he said.

"The ketchup's in the pantry!"

"No—Mandy—wait!"

I stopped, but I didn't turn around.

"Look," he said behind me. "I thought, since we were getting along now, you'd think you were supposed to hang around with me all the time."

I turned to look at him. "You really thought that? Why would you raise this cool sister and then look for reasons not to trust her to always be cool?"

When I got to my room, I didn't slam the door, so it was still open when, about an hour later, Michael poked his head in.

"Hey, Sis. I'm still hungry," he said. "Wanna go get a milkshake?"

"You buying?" I asked.

"Why? Don't you have money?"

"Yeah, I've got some."

"Really?"

"Yeah," I said.

He looked at me innocently. "Can I have some?"

I snorted and threw a pillow at him. "In your dreams!"

A grin broke over his face as he tossed it back. "Meet me in the Jeep."

Then he gave me a look—a look that said, *I'm sorry and I respect you and I'm glad you're my kid sister.*

I didn't just think it. I kept it in my heart.

Be devoted to one another in brotherly love. Honor one another above yourselves.

Romans 12:10

God Speaks:

Humility and the lack of a self-serving ego is a sign that I am at work in your life.

My Dad

I t was raining the day I met my real father. I was careful to call him my "biological father" around Ted. He's my adopted dad.

It probably wouldn't have bothered Ted (Dad). After all, he'd helped me locate Jack Darnell through the adoption agency.

"OK, Barry, we'll be looking for Tidwell Roofing on Rock Boulevard," Dad said. "It shouldn't be too hard to find, huh? How many streets can there be in a town this size?"

Dad hadn't stopped talking in the two hours since we'd left home. I, on the other hand, was doing a silent inner balancing act between uncontrollable excitement and undefined dread.

I watched a raindrop that had just smashed into the windshield make its way slowly down the glass, tracing a path to who knows where. That was just how I felt. Moving right into the unknown as if I knew what I was doing, with no real idea how it was going to end up.

"This is the place, Bar'," Dad said.

I pulled my eyes from the windshield.

"He said to wait in the main office. He'll pick you up when he gets off work—" he glanced at his watch, "in about five minutes. Barry?"

"Yeah?"

"I hope you find out what you need to know, Son."

I looked into the strong, square face I'd been looking to for support since I could focus my eyes.

He couldn't tell me what I needed to know this time. And he couldn't take away the fear of what I might find out.

I sat down in the main office to wait and tried to keep from clawing a hole through my jeans.

I hadn't thought seriously about finding my "real" father until we'd started studying genetics in biology.

"Some of who you are is the way your parents have raised you," Miss Lamb had told us. "But much of it is the genes you were born with."

In the "nurture" department, I'd done pretty well. My adopted parents had brought me up to be a Christian. God was in everything I did—from pitching baseballs to cranking out term papers.

But Miss Lamb had gotten me thinking about the "nature" part. What raw material was I cut from?

It had taken six months for Dad to find out my biological mother had been killed in an accident twelve years before and that my biological father was working as a roofer just two hours away from where we lived. Dad had even been cool about arranging this meeting. That was the way he was. The question was—what was the way I was?"

"You Barry?"

I jerked my head up.

My father stood in the doorway.

It hit me right away that he had about a foot and a good eighty pounds on me.

Beyond that, I couldn't tell you much about those first thirty seconds. For me it was like the unveiling of a statue that had stood covered in the corner of my mind for sixteen years.

He stuck out his hand. "Jack Darnell," he said.

"Barry Mitchell," I said.

"So—"

"Yeah—"

"You want something to eat?"

"Sure." I didn't. My stomach felt like rancid cottage cheese. But I followed him to the restaurant across the street. Inside he shook the rain from his hair, Saint Bernard style, and said to the girl behind the counter, "Two, Roseanne."

"You don't want to hit the bar first?" she asked.

"I got a young friend with me."

I walked to the table with a steak knife stuck in my heart. *A young friend?* But I took a deep breath before I sat down. I'd been a son all my life. He'd only been a dad for five minutes.

"Beer, Jack?" Roseanne asked.

Jack looked at me as if the decision were mine and shook his head. "I understand you've been raised Christian," he said when she'd walked away. "I don't want to offend you or nothin'."

There was an awful silence until the salads arrived. He drowned his with French dressing and punched it savagely with a fork. I knew I was making him squirm, staring at him the way I was. But I had to look at him, had to put things together. It struck me that he looked like a thicker, harder, slower version of the kids I snapped towels at in the locker room.

"Something wrong with your salad?" he asked.

I jumped. "No." I laughed nervously. "Hey, uh, I know this is all pretty weird, so—could you just tell me about yourself?"

I cringed. I sounded like Oprah Winfrey on a bad day. He wiped his mouth with his napkin twelve times before he started talking.

"OK—let's see—I'm doin' roofs right now, but I do a little carpentry, some plumbing—whatever I can get. Was married. Divorced now. Got two girls."

I stopped in mid-bite. "Yeah?"

"Amy and Jennifer. Six and four."

"You have pictures?" I asked.

He looked at me quizzically and shook his head. He had no idea he was talking about my sisters.

"Do you—get to see them much?" I asked.

"I usually work fifty hours a week just to pay child support," he said. "That doesn't leave much time for takin' 'em to Disneyland."

Impatiently he pounded the bottom of the ketchup bottle with his palm as Roseanne put our steaks on the table.

"You don't look like you're wantin' for anything," he said to me.

"No . . . I'm . . . I'm not."

He laughed a little. "It's a good thing because I sure don't have anything to give you."

"I'm not asking for anything!" I said. "I just—"

"Tell me about you. You play sports?" His voice was softer.

"Baseball."

"Varsity?"

"Yeah. I pitch."

"No kidding!"

"Do you play?" I asked.

"Bought season tickets for the Royals' games this year. I couldn't afford it, but what the–um—who's your team?"

"I'm usually too busy playing myself to watch much. Our varsity team was district champ this year, and now I'm on a community team for the summer. I'm bucking for a scholarship—to college."

My voice faded off as he chewed and nodded. I'd lost him. I conditioned and trained and practiced and played. My biological father sat in the stands and drank beer.

"I could've been a good ball player," he said. "But life just gets you, and before you know it, you're workin' for the dollar all the time."

"Yeah," I said.

The platters left the table, mine still half full, and the pieces of pie appeared. Jack tore into his, then looked at his watch, and I knew the evening was almost over. The desperation surged up my esophagus and out my mouth.

"Why did you give me up?" I asked. "I just need to know."

For a second his eyes flickered panic, the first emotion of any kind I'd seen on his face. Then he blinked it back.

There was more mouth wiping.

"I was eighteen," Jack finally said. "Just a couple years older than you are now. I didn't want to be tied down with a family. Neither did she. We had livin' yet to do."

He stared at his hands and then at the ceiling, but he didn't say anything else.

"Whoa—it's late," I said. I put on my student council voice and stuck out my hand. "Thanks for taking the time to meet me."

He shook my hand.

I walked out of the restaurant.

As I ran through the rain to Dad's car, I was thinking: *Jack wasn't embarrassed because he'd given me up to live his life to the fullest. He was embarrassed because he hadn't really lived his life anyway, with or without me in it. He was a thirty-four-year-old man with a face that had stopped developing character at eighteen, while the rest of his body moved on to middle age.*

Dad didn't say anything when I got in the car, but I could feel him looking at me sideways for about forty miles.

"Your father's a big fella," he said finally. "I saw him come out of the—"

"Am I an overachiever, Dad?" I blurted out.

He laughed his soft laugh. "I don't get the connection."

"Here I am working for a scholarship, trying to be this baseball star and honor student. But look at my genes. You've always told me you were raising me to be somebody special, but maybe that's somebody I can never be!"

During that monologue, Dad pulled the car off the road. A McDonald's sign lit up the front seat as he turned off the ignition. "I haven't said much during this whole thing because I knew finding your father was part of finding out who you are, and everyone has to do that somehow." He looked at me seriously. "But now I have to tell you, it really doesn't matter who I am or who Jack Darnell is."

"But he gave me my genes."

"And I taught you what to do with them. But the bottom line is, the real stuff doesn't come from either one of us fathers. It's your other Father you really need to get to know."

It took me a minute.

"He's made the plans for you, Son. He's made you everything you need to be to carry them out. Jack Darnell was a kid when you were born. He did everything he really could for you. And at this point, I've pretty much done all I can too."

Dad held my shoulder as if he were trying to squeeze his next words into it. "But God will never be finished with you. It seems to me He's the Father you're looking for to make you who you're going to be."

I turned in the seat and squinted through the dark rain at the little town we'd left behind.

"He let you bring me up," I said. "Maybe He knew down deep Jack Darnell would never say to me what you just said."

"If he didn't know that, you can bet your Heavenly Father did."

"Dad?" I asked.

"Yeah?"

"Could we get a hamburger?"

He started the ignition. "You just had dinner."

"I couldn't eat a thing back there. But right now I could go for a Big Mac and fries, maybe a shake—"

Dad laughed and pulled into the drive-thru line. Funny. I felt like I was lining up for a new life.

You received the Spirit of sonship. And by him we cry, "Abba, Father." The Spirit himself testifies with our spirit that we are God's children.

Romans 8:15-16

God Speaks:

You are on My mind every minute of every hour of every day.

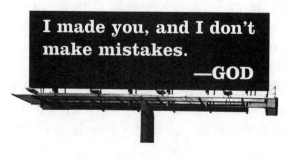

I made you, and I don't make mistakes.
—GOD

Nothing But the Truth

"That's a wrap, folks," Avis said. "Rehearsal at 3:30 P.M. tomorrow. Be there!"

"Or be square!" we answered in unison.

Justin grimaced as he and I jumped the few feet from the stage to the floor in the church hall. "When you guys pick up a phrase, you use it to death," he said.

That was Justin for you. He wasn't a geek by any means, but sometimes you'd have thought he was an adult. That, plus the chiseled good looks, had made me chairman of his fan club from the minute I started going to his church.

I'd thought landing two of the leading parts in the play would spark dating possibilities, but it had become obvious early on that the kind of sophistication he looked for in a girl kept me way out of his romance range. At least we were starting a close friendship—I could deal with that.

"You're doing a great job as Rachel," he said as we headed down the hall arm in arm.

"You're a great Jacob."

"I wanted to tell you this one thing, though."

I grinned at him expectantly. "What?"

"Your voice is so whiny it could drive the audience up the wall."

My grin faded.

"Why don't you leave the coaching to me, Justin?"

We turned to see Avis behind us. Thank heaven. I couldn't think of a thing to say to Justin, except maybe a meek, mousy "excuse me."

Avis flung her arm casually around Justin's neck. "The church is paying me to do the drama coaching, so maybe you ought to let me earn my salary."

Then with a wink for both of us, she swung out the door.

Aside from the two spots of bright pink at the tops of his cheeks, Justin didn't look fazed in the least.

"Do I really have a squeaky voice?" I asked.

He smiled in that brotherly way I loved. "I was just being honest. I thought you'd want to know. Hey, want to go to Shakey's, get a pizza?"

Honest. OK—I could do honest.

By the time we got to Shakey's, I forgot about it. The after-rehearsal get-togethers were almost the best part of doing the play.

I squeezed into a booth beside Rob Wainwright and yelled to Justin above the din, "Order me a Diet Coke!"

Rob poked me. "Diet? You're a rail already."

I took a second look at Rob. He'd only been in our youth group a couple of weeks, and I hadn't really checked him out. He was tall, even when he was sitting, and he grinned down at me.

"This is the craziest group of people I've ever seen. I come to one meeting, and they cast me as Naphtitili in some play."

"Naphtitili! But you're good at it."

Rob's brown eyes almost crinkled closed. "Yeah, I'm great at standing around in a bathrobe with a towel on my head." He punched me softly in the shoulder. "Rachel's a perfect part for you."

Justin grabbed my arm. "You ought to play Esau, though," he said.

"Why?" I asked, shooting him a sour look.

"You have a ton of hair on your arms. I never noticed that before."

I stared at them, mind racing for a retort, face pulsing.

"Just call me ape woman," I said finally. At that point, our pizza arrived, and Justin turned toward it. All I could do was blink at the back of his head. I forgot about Rob—and everybody else.

I was still hurting over it that night, and I couldn't figure out why. After all, everything Justin had said was the truth. That's the kind of Christian he was. And so adult.

If I were as mature as Justin, I thought, *I'd change those things about myself instead of pouting.* I wondered vaguely as I fell asleep how I was going to get rid of the hair on my arms.

The next day at the start of rehearsal, Avis said, "Rachel, I want to compliment you on your volume."

"Does that mean she has a big mouth?" Chuck Sawyer asked.

I let out a guffaw and smacked him. "I think I hear your mother calling you."

Rob had stepped up behind Chuck and was looking lazily down at him. Then he grinned at me. "Got any more light work for me?"

I smiled back. This boy was beginning to grow on me.

The scene we rehearsed first involved only the twelve brothers, so I propped my feet up to get a load of Rob as "Naphtitili." Justin slipped in beside me.

"I like this part with Chuck and those guys," I whispered to him. "Even if he doesn't ever get off my case."

Justin wrinkled his handsome forehead. "They tease you about being loud, but, you know, it isn't all that ladylike."

Self-consciously, I lowered my feet off the chair.

"Yesterday at Shakey's," he went on, "you were really rowdy."

I nodded stupidly. One more thing to work on in myself, and I was going to overload.

The play opened Friday. Thursday afternoon the hall was teeming with the confusion of dress rehearsal.

"The costume is you," Rob said to me.

"Oh. Thanks," I said absently.

"Me—I look like I'm headed for bed."

I wished he'd go, then. I needed to find a safety pin to keep my veil from coming open over my arms.

"Are you nervous?" he asked. "I'm a basket case, and I don't even have to say anything."

My eyes scanned the room for somebody on the costume committee.

"Hey, there's a cast party after the show. Maybe we could go together."

I stared at him, only vaguely aware that he'd even been talking.

"I wish it were over," I said. "I hate this."

I don't know which one of us turned away first.

In Justin's and my first scene, no sooner was my opening line out of my mouth than Avis was cupping her hand around her ear.

"These sheep belong to my father, Laban," I said again, my voice rising to a screech.

"I am your father's kinsman and Rebekah's son," Justin said.

I looked at him blankly. "Oh," I said.

He rolled his eyes. "The line is 'I will run and tell my father.'"

Avis's heels clicked toward the stage. "Beth, is there a problem?"

You mean aside from the fact that my voice sounds like a fingernail on a blackboard, I thought, *and I feel like I have hair growing all over my body?* I shook my head glumly.

"Start from Justin's cue, and let's try to loosen up."

She didn't say anymore, but I could feel the disappointment in her eyes as that scene—and the rest of the ones I was in—dragged on. I skipped her closing comments and retreated to the restroom. By the time I was dressed, she met me at the door.

"There's something bothering you," she said. "Have I discouraged you somehow?"

"No!" I said, "You've been great. I'm OK."

"No, you aren't, Beth. I chose you to play Rachel because you're a natural on the stage. But for the last several rehearsals, you've been like R2D2 up there. That doesn't happen for no reason."

I didn't answer.

"I can't force it out of you," she said, "but I have the very strong feeling you've been getting some unofficial coaching on the side."

Miserably, I watched her walk away. It would be different if the "coaching" had been out of spite. But all I could hear was Justin saying, "I'm only being honest."

"You OK?" It was Rob again. I answered without looking at him.

"If one more person asks me that, I'm going to scream. I'm fine!"

He lifted his hands in surrender and walked off.

The call the next night was at 6:30, and when I arrived at 6:31, Justin was outside the girls' restroom ready to pounce.

"Where've you been?" he said in lieu of hello. Then his face softened a little. "You going to be OK tonight?"

I swung abruptly toward the costume rack. "Probably not!" I said over my shoulder. "I'll probably blow the entire show."

I could feel him staring after me.

I scraped the hangers viciously across the bar. Just as my hand closed over Rachel's veils, I heard the voices from behind the brothers' robes.

"I thought she was a neat girl at first. I was planning to ask her to the cast party," Rob said.

"So why don't you?"

"Because she's a snob."

"Nah—Beth's just wrapped up in Jus-tin." Chuck's voice stiffened mockingly. I clutched at the veil and stood there, frozen.

"You got that wrong," Rob said. "She's wrapped up in herself. Every time I've tried to talk to her this week, man, she's looked at me like I was a piece of Saran Wrap—and then popped off at me. That's the mark of a woman with herself on her mind."

A robe was lifted off the rack, and I jerked away, but behind me, I could still hear Rob.

"When I joined this church, I thought the girls would be different, being Christians and all that stuff. She's as stuck up as the rest of them."

I picked up my costume and walked numbly to the restroom to change. A few minutes later, I stepped out as Rachel. When I looked up, Justin was coming toward me.

"Stay out of my face," I said tightly. "I don't need you hurting my feelings anymore, so if you have additional advice, just keep it to yourself, OK?"

"When did I ever hurt your feelings?"

"The squeaky voice? The big mouth? The hairy arms? Does any of that ring a bell?"

Justin's lips twitched. "I was just being honest, Beth. Isn't that what this play is about? God hates lips that lie—remember?"

I was clenching my teeth. "But it isn't lying when you keep something to yourself that really can't help somebody."

"If you can't take it—"

"No—I can't afford to take it. Because I got so tied up in trying to correct all the things you said were wrong with me, I missed a chance to make somebody else see what Christians are really like—"

"Is there a problem?" Avis's calm voice eased over us. I tugged at my veils, and Justin studied me openly. Only the two pink spots at the tops of his cheeks made him look any different than usual, but suddenly he was anything but handsome to me.

"No problem, Avis," I said.

Her eyes passed between the two of us, and a gleam of understanding came into them.

"Good," she said. "Then let's do a show."

The brothers headed for backstage, and as Rob passed, I started to go after him.

"Beth!" Justin said. "What's wrong with you?"

"Nothing's wrong with me, Justin," I said over my shoulder—in my wonderful, loud, squeaky voice. "Nothing at all."

You created my inmost being; you knit me together in my mother's womb. I praise you because I am fearfully and wonderfully made; your works are wonderful, I know that full well.

Psalm 139:13-14

God Speaks:

There isn't anyone on the face of the earth that is just like you. You are an absolute original. I know because I made you myself.

Love one another.
Is that so hard?
—GOD

I Can Pencil You in at Midnight

My Nikes squealed across the linoleum for the back door at 7:20 A.M. My mother's voice screeched them to a halt.

"Ben—!"

"I have to meet Trish and Chad at 7:30," I called over the shoulder that was propping open the screen door. "We've got to get our act together for this fund-raising thing for church. I don't have time—"

"You need to eat," she said. "I don't want some skinny, little, shriveled-up kid for a son." She squeezed one of my biceps. "We agreed to your quitting wrestling—not to your getting puny."

The phone rang, and she went for it. I took the opportunity to make my break.

She shook her head at me, but I was out of there. I barely heard her saying, "Matt, honey, he's out the door for school. He's kind of hard to catch up with these days—"

I took off at a semi-trot, glancing at my watch.

OK, 7:30 A.M. That gave me about fifteen minutes to talk to Trish and Chad about the car wash, and I'd still have another ten to do that night's algebra homework. If I didn't get it done that morning, there was no way I could work with the latchkey kid program that afternoon and go to the evangelism training session they were having that night.

I really wanted to do that. About six months ago, even after being a Christian all my life, it had suddenly dawned on me what it all meant—that it wasn't something you put on Sunday morning with the tie your Mom makes you wear. It was like another skin. I'd even given up wrestling, so I could devote more time to church. Now that my second skin fit pretty well, I figured I was ready to start letting it rub off on other people. Yeah, I had to get to that witnessing thing.

It was 7:34 A.M. Trish was two minutes late, Chad four. I looked at my watch as he tossed his books on the bench.

"You guys got anything to eat?" Chad asked. "I'm starved."

"You're late," I said, opening my calendar book.

"Yeah. Late *and* starved." Chad wiggled his eyebrows.

"Let's just get on with this, *shall we?*" I said. "I've got stuff to do."

Trish sighed and opened her notebook.

By the time we got the car wash planned, I had ten minutes to whip out fifteen equations. I was just hunching over my notebook when somebody said, "Hey."

It was Matt, muscles rippling as he clutched his history book. I put down my pencil and stuck out my hand. He was my best friend, and I hadn't really even seen him for two weeks.

"Hey, man!" I said. "What's happening?"

He shrugged his wide wrestler's shoulders and pulled a hand across the back of his twenty-inch neck. Matt *was* wrestling at our school.

"What's going on?" I said, slanting my eyes nervously to the page and back up again.

"Bunch of stuff." Matt sat on the end of the bench.

"Like what?" OK—five minutes for Matt, and I could probably still get the problems done.

He looked around the courtyard, which was quickly filling up with kids. "Can we go somewhere else and talk?"

I thumped my algebra book restlessly. "I really have to get these done," I said. "I've got a church thing after school and another one tonight—"

Matt shrugged again and tossed out a grin. "Guess I'll have to have my secretary call your secretary so we can do lunch."

I grinned back. "I can't do lunch," I said. "I have to make a bunch of phone calls."

His grin was starting to fade a little, but he managed a half-chuckle. "You think you can pencil me in somewhere?"

"Come on, man, of course!" I said. "What's your schedule today?"

He looked at me blankly. Matt was about as likely to have a schedule in a calendar book as he was to own a pair of panty hose.

The warning bell rang.

"Catch me later. We'll talk," I said. He nodded.

It was 11:00 A.M., and the algebra problems still weren't done. I'd gone to three classes, checked Trish's posters, and was on my way to the phone to call Pastor Wallen to be sure we could use the church parking lot Saturday when Matt caught me.

"Got a minute?" he asked.

"Got a second," I said.

He wasn't grinning, but he wasn't mad either. "OK," he said. "I'll try you later."

"Before sixth," I called to him as his broad shoulders disappeared down the hall.

It was 1:05 P.M. Before sixth. The only place I could find to get those last pain-in-the-neck equations done was crouched outside the classroom door.

I'd just squatted down when I felt Matt standing over me.

"I really have to talk to you, man," he said.

I stood up and punched his steel-band arm—and practically broke my knuckles.

"So let's talk," I said. I could probably get the problems done while Mr. Hess was taking the roll.

Matt shook his head. There wasn't a grin within a block of his face. But he still wasn't mad. Matt never got mad.

"I mean really talk," he said. "Like for an hour."

I tried not to look at my watch or my calendar book. But an hour?

"That's all I need," he said.

I grinned at him. "OK," I said. "I can pencil you in about midnight tonight."

He nodded solemnly. "OK. Call me."

I could feel my face contorting in disbelief. "I was just kidding, man!"

"I wasn't," he said.

OK, 2:05 P.M. I headed for my locker. Get to Latchkey. Then maybe slip out a little early to get the rest of those problems done.

I opened the locker door, and a piece of paper fell out. I unfolded it to Matt's unmistakable scrawl.

"I know you have a lot of stuff going on," he'd written, "and I understand. But I have to talk to you. Don't forget to call me at midnight."

In the three years we'd been friends, in the two years we'd eaten, slept, and inhaled wrestling together, Matt had never written me a note. Call me a slow learner, but for the first time that day, I realized Matt must really have something on his mind. I wasn't going to wait until midnight to call him. I'd call him—between Latchkey and the evangelism meeting, maybe.

At 6:30 P.M., I was still at the church with the Delaski twins. Their mother had to work late, and I was going to be playing Nintendo with them, probably until my eyes dissolved in their sockets or she showed up, whichever came first.

It was 7:02 P.M. before Mrs. Delaski showed up and dragged the twins off. I switched off the TV and hurried to the meeting room. The training session was supposed to start at seven, but the usual before-getting-settled-down chatter was going on when I came in. Chad was the center of attention in a huddle of kids.

"They said the veins in his neck were standing out," he was saying. "I guess he just totally lost control."

"Why?" somebody else asked.

"The wrestling coach said the wrong thing or something, and he just lost it."

I turned around with a jerk.

"Who?" I asked.

"Matt," Chad said.

"What happened?"

"He went to wrestling practice and was doing his thing. Coach just came over to, y'know, to tell him he was messing up a hold or something, and Matt exploded. Started yelling at Coach. Took a mat and shoved it across the room."

Trish nodded. "Tony called me when I got home tonight. He was there. It was ugly."

"What's gonna happen to him?" Chad asked.

"It's got to go through a bunch of people in the office," Trish said, "but Tony said the coach told Matt he was off the team—for good."

It was 7:16 P.M., and I'd been staring at the pastor for nine minutes. All I could see was Matt blowing the one thing that meant the most to him because he was hurting, and his best friend hadn't even had time to let him talk about it.

At 7:18 P.M. I went for the door. Nobody came after me—although I knew the next day somebody would want to know why. I'd suddenly decided I didn't want to learn about evangelism.

But that was just the point. I did want to—where it counted.

I used the phone in the church office. At first Matt's mom wouldn't let me talk to him. She said he was grounded—and from the way her voice was shaking, I was pretty sure Matt losing his place on the wrestling team had only been the top of a whole pile of stuff. Stuff I didn't even know was happening in their family—and I should have.

"Please, Mrs. Flint," I said. "I really have to talk to him. Just for a minute."

She finally handed him the phone. "Yeah?" he asked.

I took in a breath. "Hey, man. I hear you had a little trouble today. You wanna talk?"

There was a chilly silence. Then he said, "It isn't midnight yet. You sure you got time?"

His voice took me down worse than any move he'd ever used on me in wrestling. I was flat on the mat. The Matt who never got mad was mad.

"Yeah. I got time," I said. "I always had time. I just didn't take it. You wanna talk now?"

He snorted. "You pencilin' me in?"

"No, man. Can I come over?"

The last thing he did before we hung up was grunt, but I took it for a yes.

At 7:30 P.M. I was knocking on his door. We were going to talk. What time we'd finish was anybody's guess. But, man, I didn't care what time it was. That was a miracle, I think.

"A new command I give you: Love one another. As I have loved you, so you must love one another. By this all men will know that you are my disciples, if you love one another."

John 13:34-35

God Speaks:

Genuine love is a choice that you make to put another's needs above your own.

I don't play favorites.
—GOD

Playing Favorites

L inzee tossed her lifeguard bag on the kitchen counter. She'd just spent the afternoon guarding the kiddy pool at the swim club, and she was hot, tired, and thirsty. She opened the fridge and let out a yell. "Who took my bottle of juice?"

Linzee's mom appeared, followed by Sarah, Linzee's six-year-old sister.

"What's all the yelling about?" Mrs. Addison asked.

"Mom, you gave Sarah my juice!" Linzee yelled as she spotted her little sister holding her drink.

"Oh, dear," Mrs. Addison sighed as Sarah took a quick step behind her to hide from Linzee's wrath. "I'm sorry, but Sarah kept whining about how much she wanted it. I finally gave it to her, so I could have some peace."

"She always gets what she wants just because she's the youngest," Linzee accused. "You're always playing favorites."

"Linzee that's not fair," her mom replied. "I don't mean to play favorites, but sometimes it's easier to say yes just to keep the peace. I'll buy you a bottle of juice the next time I'm at the store."

"Forget it," Linzee mumbled as she headed to her room. "I wouldn't want any special treatment."

"Linzee—"

Linzee slammed her door to block out the reprimand she knew was coming.

It's not fair that Sarah gets everything she wants just because she's the youngest, she thought as she banged around her room, trying to vent some of her frustration before she headed out to the youth-group council meeting that afternoon. *Mom should treat us all the same.*

A few minutes later, Linzee yanked her door open and went back to the kitchen.

"I'm going to Colleen's," she announced as she headed for the door. "I'll be home for dinner."

"Hopefully in a better mood than when you left," her mom replied.

The meeting had already started by the time Linzee got there. Besides Colleen, there were Greg and Solomon, who guarded with Linzee at the pool. "So what'd I miss?" she asked, plopping down in the circle.

"We were talking about our next service project," Greg told her. "We'd like to tackle something different than our usual nursing home visit. We want something we can commit to for a while instead of a one-time deal."

Linzee nodded. "What have you guys come up with?"

"Well," Solomon said slowly. "I know some people who just moved downtown to start an inner-city ministry. They need volunteers to pitch in with everything from cleanup to helping with kids' programs to volunteering in the soup kitchen to—"

"Wait a minute," Linzee interrupted. "You want to go downtown for a service project?"

Solomon nodded. "I thought we should consider it. People there need God as much as anyone else."

"Couldn't it be dangerous?" Linzee asked. "Shouldn't we leave that to professionals or somebody?"

"Somebody besides us, you mean?" Solomon asked.

Linzee squirmed. "I'm just uncomfortable with—Oh, I don't know. I'm not sure I can relate to poor people or homeless people. It feels weird, okay?"

"Scared to step out of your comfort zone?" Colleen asked.

"A little," Linzee admitted.

"Me too," Colleen said with a smile. "So maybe this is one project we'll have to trust God on."

"Dave, my friend down there, has strict guidelines for all his volunteers," Solomon interrupted. "Everything is done in teams, there's always an adult involved, and volunteers aren't allowed in unsafe neighborhoods. And all teen volunteers have to get their parents' permission."

"How about if we think about it and meet again at the end of the week?" Colleen suggested. "If we decide we'd like to try it, we'll get permission and go forward."

"All in favor?" Greg said, raising his hand.

All the others raised their hands too.

For the next couple of days, Linzee couldn't get the project out of her mind. *Why didn't we pick a kids' camp or something easy?* she thought. *Why this?*

On Thursday, Linzee had to work again. She took her place at the kiddy pool and smiled as she saw Solomon guarding the bigger pool on the other side of the fence. She caught his eye and waved. He smiled and waved back.

At break, Solomon came over. "So, what are you thinking about?"

Linzee raised her eyebrows. "I'm sure you know."

"Good," Solomon said with a smile. "Then can I ask you a question?"

"Sure."

"Are there any kids in this pool right now whom you wouldn't save if they were drowning?"

Linzee looked at him in amazement. "That's a stupid question. Of course not!" "

So as a lifeguard, you don't play favorites?"

Linzee gave a rueful laugh. *Where've I heard that before?* she thought. "No, as I lifeguard, I don't play favorites," she said. "But I guess what you're getting at is that I do play favorites when it comes to this service project, right?"

"Well," Solomon said slowly, "I could be wrong, but it looks that way to me. What I don't understand is how you choose who has the chance to be saved from drowning spiritually and who doesn't? Is it by how people look, where they live, whom they hang with?"

"Solomon, you ask hard questions."

"I know," Solomon said.

Linzee looked thoughtfully at her friend. "I'll have to think about that."

"That's all I ask," Solomon said. "See you at the meeting tomorrow."

The next day Linzee took her place in her circle of friends.

"Everyone had time to think about this?" Greg asked.

The group nodded.

"Linzee? How about you?" he asked.

"Something that happened with my little sister helped me decide—and talking to Solomon," she told them. "They both helped me realize how bad it feels when someone ignores how you feel or treats you unfairly."

The group was quiet.

"I realized I can't play favorites with God's love or His message. I vote we go downtown."

The rest of the group nodded.

"Who knows, Linzee," Solomon said with a grin. "This may become your favorite new service project."

Faith in Christ Jesus is what makes each of you equal with each other.

Galatians 3:28 CEV

God Speaks:

There isn't anyone, anywhere whom I love more or less than I love you. Let the reality of that statement sink into your heart and mind today.

Portraits of Me

I t seemed as though I needed more and more privacy these days. That was funny to me as I ducked into the attic with my photo album. Solitude had never been something I wanted— until six months ago.

I opened the album to put in some new pictures. But there were some old ones I wanted to look at first.

There was the one taken by Uncle Shea himself: Ryan, my younger brother, and me, sitting on the blue tractor. As I stared at the picture, that day came back to me in vivid detail—even the annoying sound of my brother's complaining. . . .

"Can you get *her* off now?" Ryan had whined. "It's my turn to plow with you."

I scowled, but I let Uncle Shea help me down.

"Sweet dreams," he said, as I marched away toward the orchard. Riding the tractor was OK, but Irish Hill—as Uncle Shea called his farm—was full of other dreams for me.

I strolled up and down the aisles of peach trees, pretending I was a Southern girl running from the Confederate soldiers because I'd set my father's slaves free.

Then I climbed on the corral rail and let the horses nuzzle their velvety mouths against my palms. I was, of course, the first eight-year-old to rescue horses from the clutches of horse thieves.

Finally I threw myself down beside the pond and listened to the ducks muttering to each other. Lying on my side, I could see the rows of trees, rolling over Irish Hill and as far away as my little mind could imagine. If only I were an orphan farm girl, running home from school to harvest my beans.

Even through the mist of my heroic daydreams, the chickens bickered across the yard. Esther, the cow, let out a long, contented moo-sigh. The sun made my hair hot, the honeysuckle made my nose happy, and I was content. I knew if I didn't remember this very moment, it might go away, never to be caught again. . . .

But I did forget. We moved three thousand miles from the farm that fall, and we didn't get back to Irish Hill.

Actually, my parents did. I didn't—until recently.

They went the summer I was fifteen, but I'd chosen cheer-leading camp.

There were plenty of pictures of me in my rah-rah outfit. I zeroed in on the one taken at a student-council meeting.

"It's just so *us!*" my best friend, Paige, had squealed over that photo. "You, me, Andy—may the Force be with us!"

"The Force": that's what they called us because we three, plus about five other kids, "ran" the school.

"OK," Andy had said that day, rapping his gavel on the library table. He smiled his cockeyed smile at a freshman in the front row, and she swooned, which was something he always said disgusted him.

"Games for pep rally," he began. "Where's the committee report?"

"Here," said a sophomore, whose name escaped me.

"OK—uh—yeah, go ahead." Her name escaped him too.

"We thought we could start with a class competition where we have, like, stuffed models of the other team's mascot at the other end of the gym, and we do a relay where—"

"I never heard of that game," one of us interrupted.

"We invented it," the sophomore said.

"What about passing those miniature footballs with your neck?" Paige asked. She giggled and nudged Andy.

"But none of the shy kids will participate in that," said the sophomore.

"Too bad for them," Andy said flippantly. "All in favor of the pass-the-football relay?"

It passed.

That was the way we got things done throughout the school. We decided who sat at our lunch table, what was OK to wear, what was OK to say, and whom it was OK to be friends with. It was a heady sensation to know freshman watched wistfully from their lockers as we adjusted the shoulder pads in our cheer-leading sweaters.

God must have done a lot of shuddering over me in those days. I think it was a God thing that my parents dragged me back to Georgia for a visit at the end of last summer. Cheerleading camp and the State Student-Council Conference were over. I didn't have an excuse. And Uncle Shea had cancer.

I flipped to that page in the album. The picture was an "after" shot of Irish Hill. More "after" than I knew at the time.

We'd arrived at night. I stumbled out to the porch around noon the next day, blinking against the sun. Uncle Shea was there, listlessly sipping at a cup of coffee. I wasn't sure what to say to a dying man I'd adored as a little girl. While I sat on the railing searching for words, I suddenly noticed what *wasn't* there.

The horse-nickering.

The cow-sighs.

The chicken-bickering and the duck-muttering.

I leaned over the railing. "Wasn't there a pond over there? And the cow, Esther—where's Esther? Did she die? She must've been old."

"Colleen," Uncle Shea said. He set down his coffee. "I don't have the farm anymore. Just the house and an acre."

"But—" I didn't finish but pointed to the fields that rolled before us as far as they ever had. That's when I saw the machines, the hulking masses of metal and motion that moved slowly over the dirt where the blue tractor once had been.

"A big corporation owns it now," he said. "This and several other farms."

"You *sold* Irish Hill?" I said, my voice pointing a prosecuting finger.

"I didn't have a choice," he said. "I couldn't make a go of it."

How had I missed that information? There must have been phone calls and conversations at our dinner table. But I was probably cheering at a game or not listening.

But I wanted to listen now.

Uncle Shea spent the rest of the afternoon telling me about the pain of giving up the farm. But he also told me about friends from his church who had been there to help. He said that if it hadn't been for them, he might have given up hope for good. At one point, he looked at me and said, "I think of you as that kind of person. You always had such dreams. I thought you'd grow up and save the world."

"I guess I didn't know it was in trouble," I replied.

"You have to know," he said. "You're the future. The world needs people who have the guts to do something about it."

For the next week, I mostly sat on the porch with Uncle Shea and found out about the world's agony. He never claimed to have the answers, but we talked about homelessness and AIDS and drugs and what he thought could be done about them.

"God's shaking His head," he told me. "He wants us to do something. Don't forget that."

To be sure I wouldn't, I went out to the porch early in the morning our last day there and took a picture of the orchard. I wanted to remember the place where I had dreamed and where I had finally decided to wake up and do something. I didn't know what issue was most important to deal with. But at least I knew what *wasn't* important anymore.

I pulled a new photo out of the envelope. My seventeenth birthday. Just last week. I was all by myself—not even Paige was there. A few days before, she had turned to me in the rest room, hands on hips, and said, "You want us to raise money for AIDS research instead of buying new cheerleading sweaters?"

"Well—yeah," I said.

She flung her backpack over her shoulder. "You're gonna lose out if you don't drop this save-the-world stuff."

"Lose out on what?" I asked.

"State Student Council for one thing. Andy's thinking of pushing for someone else to go because he says you're going to give the school a bad name."

"Miss out on the drunken parties?" I responded. "And standing in front of the mirror for hours so I can look totally awesome for some guy who's nothing but an Andy clone? I don't mind missing that!"

Paige stared at me. "Fine," she said. "Stay home and stress out over the *poor and needy.*" And then she pushed out the rest room door and let it slap closed on our friendship. That afternoon, I turned in my cheerleading outfit.

It was downhill with the Force after that, especially after Uncle Shea died in November.

The day after we'd gotten the news, I'd gathered the courage to propose at Student Council that we start a school project to help the homeless, instead of spending all our money on electing a Winter Faire King. I got to the lunch table that very *day* and found a sophomore girl in my usual chair, listening to Andy describe how he imagined the Winter Faire dance. She was swooning.

It was kind of OK. You don't miss people once you find out they didn't fill up your life anyway.

I flipped through the pictures in the envelope and pulled out one more.

I'd taken it during lunch, the day after my birthday. I'd started bringing my brown-bag lunch and eating out in the courtyard with whomever looked interesting. But I'd stopped that day, pulled my camera out of my bag, and snapped a shot of the Force huddled at their table.

Looking at it, I didn't feel as left out as I thought I would. Maybe it was because they all looked like strangers I'd never really known at all.

I closed the album. It was a relief not to have to show other people who or what to be. Who has time for that, anyway? I have a world to save.

"If anyone would come after me, he must deny himself and take up his cross and follow me. For whoever wants to save his life will lose it, but whoever loses his life for me and for the gospel will save it. What good is it for a man to gain the whole world, yet forfeit his soul?"

Mark 8:34-36

God Speaks:

To live life on My terms means that sometimes you must attach value to the things the world hates and hate the things the world loves.

Your secret's safe with me. —GOD

Private Property

S ix o'clock in the morning. I read over what I'd written in my journal so far—*I have a question about 'Honor your father and your mother.' Mom and Dad are incredible people. But does 'honor' mean I always have to deny who I am to please them? I'm not a clone of Michael, Gina, or Jamie. I can't be the president of every club and star on every team. I'm a contemplative person. I'll always honor God. I'll always honor my parents. But when do I—Anthony Hood—get to honor me?*

I stopped and let the stillness wrap itself around me. Quiet was rare in our house, like last night when I'd finished my homework and was lying on my bed, listening to music and thinking.

First Mom came in to collect dirty clothes and report that Dad had just called from L.A.

Then my older brother, Michael—the college junior who knows everything—made his weekly long-distance family call from Tulane. Minutes later my little brother, Jamie—the sixth-grader who knows even more than Michael—exploded into my room and started ransacking my CD cabinet.

Three plastic CD cases hit the rug behind him as he tossed them over his shoulder. I caught the fourth one with one hand and lifted him off the floor by the back of his T-shirt with the other.

"Do you think you could've asked first?" I asked with anger in my voice. "Or knocked?"

Jamie looked at me blankly. "Why?"

"Because it's my room, that's why!"

He started to go back to tearing into my collection, but I shoved him into the hall and slammed the door behind him. He tried the knob, but I was too quick for him. I had the chair wedged under the doorknob before he made the first jiggle.

I stopped gnawing on the end of my pen and added in my journal—*I don't think it's too much to ask for some privacy. Does God really expect me to let everyone intrude whenever they want to?*

"Charming outfit," Gina said dryly when I sat down at the breakfast table. "You look like an unmade bed."

I looked at Mom and waited for her to comment about my ensemble. But she set a basket on the table and said to me, "I need you to take Jamie to his soccer game after school today."

I frowned into my orange juice.

"You know your dad's out of town," Mom said, "and I have a doctor's appointment."

"What about Gina?" I asked.

"She has something to do."

"National Honor Society," Gina inserted.

"What if I have something to do?" I asked.

Gina smirked. "Like what?"

"Like I was going to meet some people at the diner, and then I was going to come home and—"

"Anthony, that's not something to do," Mom said. "That's nothing to do. Son, you spend far too much time holed up in your room. None of my other kids have ever done this much moping."

I took a deep breath. *Honor your father and your mother,* I told myself grimly.

"I'm not moping, Mom," I said with control.

"Then what are you doing?"

"I'm—"

"I'd be so much happier if you were out getting involved in activities—"

"Like Michael and Gina did in high school," I finished for her. "None of that stuff works for me. I'm happier—"

"Doing nothing," she finished for me.

"I'm not doing 'nothing,'" I said defensively.

"Then what are you doing?"

Honor. Honor.

"Never mind," I said as I quickly scraped my chair back from the table. "I'll take him."

As I could have predicted, I hated the soccer game. Jamie's team lost, and I couldn't wait to get home.

The house was strangely quiet when we arrived. I headed for my room, my journal, my music, and hopefully some peace. The door was ajar when I got there. My shade had been pulled up, and the late afternoon sun silhouetted my mother at my desk—reading my journal.

"What are you doing?"

She didn't jump guiltily or slap my private writings closed and hide the book behind her back. In fact, she looked me as if she'd never seen me before.

"Interesting reading, Anthony," she said in a flat tone.

"That's mine!" I said through my teeth. "Can't I have anything that's just mine?"

She stared. "I came in to put your laundry away. This was lying open on your desk, right where anyone could see it."

"You had no right to read my journal!"

"I'm your mother, Anthony. Of course I had a right."

"I have a right to my privacy!"

"Then why all this need for sneaking around?"

"What sneaking around?"

"The shades pulled down. The door always closed, locked."

"I can't lock it, or believe me I would."

"We don't lock doors in this house. We share with each other in this family. You can share anything with us, Anthony!"

"I don't want to! I have to share my shirts, my CDs, my breakfast, my time!" I slammed the journal down on the bed. "But I won't share my thoughts!"

That seemed to take her breath away. And then she brushed past me and out of my room. I slammed the door behind her.

I'd always wanted quiet, and that night I got it. Gina came into my room just to stare through me before she took Jamie out for pizza. He curled his lip at me and said, "Mom cried."

I retrieved my journal from the bed where I'd thrown it, but I wasn't sure I could write in it. It had been my last vestige of privacy, and now even it had been violated.

Was I supposed to say, "Oh, that's OK, Mom. Help yourself." How could I honor their right to invade my space and judge me when I don't think they have that right!

But God says to honor them. I just don't know what "honor" means.

"Is that what you do all those hours you spend up here? You write in there?" Mom was standing in the doorway with a plate of brownies. I had the feeling she'd been there awhile.

"Sometimes," I said without looking at her.

"What else do you do, then?" she asked.

"I do my homework and stuff. And sometimes I pray. And then I think while I'm listening to music."

"Think about what? I just want to know, Anthony. My other kids tell me things. You don't."

"I'm not like your other kids! I can't just go out there and plunge into life like Michael and Gina and Jamie. I go out and get a little of it on me, and then I come back and examine it. That's just the way I am."

She leaned over and put her hand on my arm. "That scares me," she said. "You are so different."

I pulled my arm away. "Why is that bad? I've always been a good son. I make good grades. I play by the rules. I don't talk back. Why can't I just be me?"

"That's just it, Anthony," she said. "I don't even know who you are. I saw your book there with your writing in it, and I thought I could find out more. I didn't think I was doing anything wrong."

She waved a frustrated hand toward the brownies. "That's a peace offering," she said in a wobbly voice

"Thanks," I mumbled.

She stood up. "I don't understand you, honey," she said, "but I love you. I guess I just want you to do the same for me."

"OK, Mom," I said.

She stopped at the hall and closed my door behind her.

I opened my journal and wrote.

Honor your father and your mother: that means love them, I guess. God doesn't expect me to always understand them or be like them or accept everything they do. He just expects me to love them. I think I can do that.

My salvation and my honor depend on God; he is my mighty rock, my refuge. Trust in him at all times, O people; pour out your hearts to him, for God is our refuge.

Psalm 62:7-8

God Speaks:

You can be real with Me. There is nothing you can say that I don't already know and nothing that will make Me love you any less.

I still create rainbows.
—GOD

Raindrops and Rainbows

It's spring again—time for raindrops and rainbows, Mom says. Time for April showers to bring May flowers, my little sister, Kelli, says. They both love spring.

Not me.

Rain makes me nervous. Sometimes I think I'd like to skip this season entirely or maybe move to the desert where it's usually dry.

I really felt that way last spring. That was when God remembered the raindrops but forgot the rainbows. At least it felt that way.

A year ago, Kelli's April showers turned into ten inches of rain in just a couple of hours. It didn't bring May flowers. It brought floods. Half the people in our town had houses under water. The other half were scared theirs would be.

When the rain started that day, it didn't seem like any big deal. But then it just kept on raining—as it did with Noah during the Great Flood. One minute we were watching the guy from

Channel 9 telling us about severe thunderstorms and the possibility of floods, and the next minute the Ohio River was lapping at our door. I'd never seen water come up so fast.

I guess when you live by a river, you should be prepared for floods, but I wasn't. When the policeman knocked on our door and told us we had to get out, Mom handed me some photo albums, while she took family pictures off the walls. Kelli ran for one of her dolls. That's all we left with.

The policeman said the Red Cross was setting up a shelter in the high school and that we should head there. That's where Dad met us later that day. It felt strange to be sitting on a cot in the gym while the river swallowed my town. Finally we couldn't see the town anymore—just rooftops.

Through all of it, I was amazed at my parents' faith. Every night before Kelli went to bed, we'd hold hands, and Mom and Dad would thank God for keeping our family safe. They also asked Him to help us through the days that were to come. I knew we'd need it, but I wasn't sure if God would deliver.

It seemed like it took forever, but the day finally came when we could go to see our house. On the drive there, Dad gave Mom's hand a squeeze. "Be strong," he told her. She nodded and tried to smile.

Our house was a mess. The damage was so bad that the police had it roped off and wouldn't let us inside.

"Sorry folks. It's for your own safety," the officer said.

We stood there not knowing what to say or do. Mom had tears sliding down her cheeks. Dad looked sad and tired.

I know that everything we have is given to us by God, but I have to admit I never thought we'd lose it all. I couldn't believe I was standing there with no place to live and no clothes to wear but the ones I had on. *God, are You there?* I wondered. *We need You.*

My parents would have told me that was a foolish question. They would've said that even in this, God was in control. It didn't feel like it to me. God felt far away. I was glad my parents had faith because mine was wavering.

During the days that followed, Dad filled his time with meetings, paperwork, and phone calls. He wanted to get us back on our feet as soon as possible. We moved in with my grandma who lived in a part of town that wasn't flooded. Since the schools were still closed, Mom, Kelli, and I spent a lot of time helping friends and neighbors whose homes had been damaged but not destroyed. Helping others felt good, but it felt bad that I wasn't doing more for my own family.

One night I'd had it. I was tired of living with my grandma, tired of sleeping in someone else's bed, tired of wearing someone else's clothes. "How much longer do we have to go through this?" I asked at dinner. "When do I get my life back?"

Mom laid her hand on my shoulder and looked me in the eyes. "God is holding us in the palm of His hand."

I stared at her. *What kind of answer was that?* I wondered. I wanted a timetable, and she was talking about God.

After all we'd been through, Mom still believed God was taking care of our family. I wasn't sure if I should admire her faith or laugh at it. *If this is how God's going to take care of us, I want to hire someone else for the job,* I thought.

Yet who would I hire? Myself? I almost laughed out loud. I knew too well the results of wrestling my life out of God's hands because I thought I could do a better job. Whenever I had tried to live life my way, I quickly realized it was the wrong way. Before long I'd be back telling God I'd messed up and asking Him to please take over again.

Mom's words made me do some thinking. I knew the answer to my question came down to a matter of faith. If I could trust

God to be faithful in the small areas of my life, why couldn't I trust Him in the bigger areas?

Okay, God, You lead, and I'll follow, I thought as I looked out at a starry sky. At that moment, I joined my family in believing God had the best in store for us. I knew following His way wouldn't be easy, but I also knew it was the only way to go.

These days when it rains, I still get nervous, but I realize the rain is a good reminder of God's promises to my family and me. In the year that's passed, I've found God faithful. In a few months, we'll move into our new home.

I look at life from a new perspective now. Sure I see the raindrops, but I know the rainbows can't be far behind.

We know that God is always at work for the good of everyone who loves him.

Romans 8:28 CEV

God Speaks:

I am always there to see you through even the darkest night and lead you to a brighter tomorrow.

Ready to Leave

"Do you have any homework tonight, Steve?"

"Does a monkey have bad breath?"

My parents stopped in mid-bite and stared at me.

I grinned like the monkey in question and reached for the crescent rolls.

"Don't be disrespectful," Dad said.

"Sorry." I stuffed a whole roll into my mouth.

"So, do you?" my mother asked.

I choked. I was in every sophomore honors class—because I was an A student—because not only did I always have homework, I always did it without being told. So—why were they asking me?

I said, "Yes, Mom," and savagely stabbed my roast beef with my knife.

"Be sure you take out that garbage before you hit the books," Dad said.

I pushed my plate away. I took the garbage out every night. I also stacked the firewood, kept my hair cut, and never griped about going to church.

"OK," I said tightly. "May I be excused?"

"What's wrong, sweetie? Don't you feel well?" Mom asked.

"I just have a lot to do."

Dad didn't miss the edge in my voice. His eyes followed me out of the room.

"We've never had a bit of trouble with Steve," I'd heard my mother tell people.

If I was such a model kid, why did they have to be on my case twenty-four hours a day? That was a question I'd been wrestling with for about a month, with no success.

But after I played Oscar the Grouch with the trash and retreated to my room, I felt a little guilty as I slid down in my desk chair and bit into the corner of my geometry book.

My life so far had been a series of great family vacations, surprise birthday parties, and double-fudge brownies brought in when I was up late studying. My parents never missed one of my basketball games. They treated my friends like they were prodigal sons. My mother had even sewn the letter on Zach's letterman jacket because his own mom was too busy. But they were still driving me crazy!

Mom tapped on the door and stuck the phone in. "For you, honey. Zach."

As the door closed behind her, I barked, "What?" into the phone.

"You're in a good mood." I could hear the grin in Zach's voice. "What's up?"

"Parents."

"Aah."

Zach had been fighting with his folks since he was eleven. It had always baffled him that, until about a month ago, I'd always gotten along great with mine.

"Nothing you can do about it," he said. "Besides, we have something more important to discuss."

"Like what?"

"Not like what—like who. Amanda Mussatti."

My geometry book slid to the floor. "Come on. Spill it. What do you know?"

"Just that she's been mentioning your name around school. She knows who you are, and she's interested."

My mouth felt like it was full of crumpled up paper. Amanda Mussatti. Newest and best-looking girl in the sophomore class. Reddish-blonde hair. Just enough freckles. I'd wanted to get to know her since the first time I saw her in the lunch line.

"So where does that leave me?" I asked. "She isn't in any of my classes. How am I gonna—"

"Have a party. Just a couple bags of chips, a few CDs, several of your closest friends. There's nothing to it."

"Amanda Mussatti," I said with him, as a grin worked its way across my face. "Zach, my man," I said, "you're a genius."

My mother was ecstatic that I was finally showing an interest in "entertaining."

"Two bags of Doritos and a six-pack of Coke isn't 'entertaining,'" I told her, trying to keep my voice even.

"How about if I make some of your favorite brownies—kids like those. What colors do you want?"

"What color brownies?"

She giggled and pushed me out of the kitchen. "No, honey, I mean for napkins and streamers."

"Mom! No fussy stuff, OK?" I pleaded. But she was already baking a triple batch of cupcakes in her brain.

Approaching Amanda was next. Using Zach's prowess at gleaning information from the school office, I found out where her locker was. When I put my hand on the one above hers, she looked up as if she'd been expecting me, her blue eyes tilting upward at the outer corners. She was exquisite.

"Hi," she said softly.

"Hi," I whispered back—only because my voice wouldn't come up any louder.

"You're Steve."

"You're Amanda."

"Mandy."

We stared at each other until I remembered why I was there.

I asked her. She said yes.

Friday night I combed my hair eight times and tried on sixteen different shirts. I thought I looked basically cool until I got to the family room, where I was instantly deflated.

Mom had gone with Chinese lanterns and colored chains, not to mention two platters of cupcakes with frosting in "vibrant" colors and a punch bowl big enough to take a bath in, full of something green.

I was staring at it, a broken man, when Zach came in. He stared also.

"What's going on? Are your folks having a party too?"

I grunted.

When the rest of the guys arrived, they gave me a couple weird looks and then started devouring the cupcakes. The girls all squealed over the stuff, and Amanda told my mother how great the table looked.

I let out a big sigh of relief when my parents finally went back to the kitchen.

"How 'bout some music?" Zach asked loudly.

I sat on the arm of the couch beside Amanda.

"He's playing Avalon!" she said.

"Don't you like them?" I asked. It occurred to me that Christian music might not be her thing.

"I love them! Do you have any Jars of Clay?"

"Of course. You into this kind of stuff?"

"Yeah. But I didn't know you were." Her eyes looked suddenly warm.

"Anybody need more punch?" It was my mother singing out from the table. I groaned inwardly.

"There are more chips," she said, sailing back toward the kitchen. Then she stopped and looked at me. "Steve, honey, don't sit on the arm of the sofa."

"Yeah, come on, Steven, you slob!" Zach was trying to save me, but I was already dead. My mother left the room laughing, and everybody else snickered and got back to what they were doing. I went to the table and jabbed a tortilla chip into the blue-cheese dip. I didn't even want to look at Mandy and read the word "geek" in her eyes.

I could hear my mother's voice behind me again.

"I've always thought Steve had such nice friends," she was saying to somebody. "I'm glad you're one of them now."

"Thank you," said a soft voice. I was beside her and Mandy before another word could be exchanged.

"Mom, let's get some more food," I said through gritted teeth.

She preceded me into the kitchen, where Dad was sitting at the table, reading the paper.

"Mom—do you mind?"

"What, honey?"

"Not treating me like a little kid? Could you and Dad just go to bed or something?"

Dad cleared his throat.

"I've had it," I said. "I'm fifteen, and I do everything I'm supposed to do and more, but still you won't get off my case."

Dad came right out of the chair. "I don't care what the problem is, don't take that tone with your mother or me. She has been knocking herself out, so you could have this party."

I didn't have an appropriate response. I shrugged, muttered, "Sorry, Mom," and left the room.

"Where have you been?" Zach hissed in my ear. "Amanda's in the bathroom with Carrie Crane. She thinks you aren't interested."

"Terrific," I said, sinking onto the couch.

The rest of the evening basically just went by. I avoided Mandy, although Zach told me after everyone was gone that she kept looking at me.

"Right. She was probably trying to figure out how I ever make it at school without my parents there."

"I'm tellin' you, the only thing you can do about parents is tolerate 'em until you're old enough to get your own place."

I glared at him. "In three years?"

But the next morning I'd decided he was right. I started taking stuff off my bulletin board—vacation pictures, old birthday cards from my folks, a leather engraving of the Ten Commandments. With a stab, I remembered how I'd approached "Honor thy father and mother"—breakfast in bed for both of them, that kind of stuff. But the memory of "Steve, honey, don't sit on the arm of the sofa," wiped out the guilt.

I was on my way to the trash can with a bag full of memories when the phone rang. The bag dropped to the floor when I heard Mandy's voice.

"I didn't get to thank you for inviting me to the party," she said.

I felt like a worm. "Listen," I said clumsily, "I'm sorry I acted like a jerk."

"You must have really good parents," she said.

Good grief. Couldn't my parents be kept out of anything?

"To teach you such good manners," she went on. "Most guys wouldn't even bother to apologize."

"I guess."

"Your mom's nice."

I snorted. "Yeah, if you like being smothered."

She laughed softly. "You must be leaving."

"Not for another three years."

"No!" she laughed again. "Not *leaving*—leaving. Just starting to leave. In your mind."

"I don't get it." By this time I'd dropped into a chair and flung one leg over the arm, just for spite.

"Your folks still treat you like they always did, which is why you're such a neat person in the first place. But you're mentally getting yourself ready to leave someday and be out on your own. So the way they've always treated you seems babyish. It gets on your nerves."

"No joke."

"But you feel guilty when you want to pop off at them."

I was grinning. "How did you know?"

"My mother—going shopping with her used to be right up there with the dentist's drill."

"Used to be?"

"Until I learned this leaving thing. It doesn't change anything. It just helps you to understand it."

"You're going to teach it to me, of course," I said.

"Start with Luke 18. And then Mark 10. Oh, and Proverbs 6."

"Are we talking the Bible here?" I said.

There was an awkward silence. "You listen to Christian music," she said finally. "I just thought . . . "

"I am!"

She sounded relieved. "OK. So go for it."

As soon as we hung up—her soft laughter still floating around in my head—I took down a Bible, and there it was, just like she said. I was reading Proverbs 6:20-23 for the third time when my mother passed through with a stack of folded laundry.

"Hi, Mom," I said, gingerly swinging my leg off the arm of the chair.

She looked at me curiously.

"Hi, Steve," she said.

Then we smiled at each other—for the first time in a month.

"If anyone loves me, he will obey my teaching. My Father will love him, and we will come to him and make our home with him."

John 14:23

God Speaks:

With Me, it's all or nothing. When I come into your life, I don't just come to visit—I move in.

Sissyboy

Motorcycle engines roared as anxious riders revved their throttles on the starting line.

It was a perfect day for a desert race. The sky was clear with a slight breeze that would chase away dust, making the course safer and faster.

This late in the season meant the hot desert temperatures had cooled down to a comfortable level that at times even seemed a little chilly.

Jonathan had some time before his race began. He sat on his motorcycle in the pit and looked in the direction of the racer pitted next to him. "He would have to park right there!" he muttered. Rodney stepped out of his dad's motor home.

"Hey, Sissyboy," Rodney called out when he saw Jonathan.

"Ready to get creamed today?" Jonathan yelled back.

"In your dreams!" Rodney threw his leg over his bike and kick-started it almost in one fluid motion. He waved toward the starting line. "Wanna go watch the start?" he asked as he pulled on his helmet.

"Nah," Jonathan said. "You go on." He had some last-minute prep to do on his bike and was glad for the opportunity to miss spending time with Rodney.

The two had been battling all year long. Now the race for class champion had come down to this last race of the season. And Rodney had the edge.

Earlier in the year, Jonathan had chosen to miss a race to go on a missions trip with his church youth group. Rodney won that race and soared ahead of him in the point standings. They had been running only one or two points apart up until then. Jonathan had really struggled with whether or not to go on the trip, knowing it would give Rodney a strong lead.

When it came right down to it though, his commitment to God was greater than his commitment to race. He had prayed long and hard before signing up for the missions trip, aware there would be sacrifice involved, not just for himself, but for all the sponsors who helped him raise the money.

He came back from the missions trip closer to God but farther away from the number-one spot in the point standings. At the same time, he had been dubbed "Sissyboy" by Rodney, who couldn't understand how anyone could put God above motorcycle racing.

The roar of the motorcycles was replaced by sudden silence. Jonathan looked over at the starting line. The riders for this race had been given the sign to shut the bikes off.

Desert races have an element of difficulty that most motorcycle races don't have. They are "dead-engine" starts, meaning that after the green flag is dropped, the riders have to kick start their bikes before they can take off. This sometimes leaves unfortunate racers on the line, kicking a stubborn bike that refuses to start. It makes motorcycle maintenance all the more important. No matter how fast you are, if your bike doesn't start on the first or second kick, you've got problems.

The man dropped the green flag, and the deafening roar of the motorcycle engines excited Jonathan as if it were his first race all over again. Motorcycle racing was in his blood, and he watched, enthralled as the racers sped across the desert.

When the last racer was out of sight, he got off his bike and began to mix his gas and oil to prepare for his race.

"Are you sure you want to race today?"

Jonathan looked up and forced a smile.

"Did you check out the point standings after the last race?" Rodney asked.

They raced fifteen times a year, skipping the hot summer months. Their last race had been three weeks earlier.

"I saw them," Jonathan said. He held up the measuring cup and poured oil into it.

"Notice who was on top?"

"I saw you there, Rodney," Jonathan said as he poured the measured oil into the gas can and then shook the mixture together.

"One more win," Rodney said. "That's all I need."

"You don't even need to win," Jonathan admitted. "You'd have to break down for me to pass you in the points."

"At least you're a realist, Sissyboy," Rodney said. "Well, gotta get ready to earn that number-one plate. It's gonna look nice on my bike, don't you think?" he taunted as he swaggered back to his own pit.

Jonathan hoisted the heavy gas can up. While he poured the gas into his motorcycle tank, he muttered, "God, why'd You have to put such an unlikable person in my life?"

He checked his tires and spark plug, then wiped the dirt off his number plate, so the scorekeepers could read it. He had longed for the number-one plate to ride with the following year, but the only way that would happen was if Rodney didn't finish the upcoming race. Of course, in a fifty-mile desert race, that was a possibility. But more than likely, he'd be settling for number two and a year of listening to Rodney brag.

Twenty miles into his race, Jonathan sped down a wide, flat sandwash. It was the fastest part of the course, and he hoped to gain some ground on Rodney. Rodney was a little more skillful in the technical sections, but Jonathan's motorcycle was geared for high speeds, and he could fly in the straight sections.

He knew the only rider ahead of him was Rodney, and he kept his eyes glued to the trail ahead in search of that blue motorcycle. Then he saw it. But it wasn't moving.

The bike was lying in a ditch up ahead, just off the race course. It wasn't running! Jonathan had his chance!

He pinned the throttle even more as he realized he'd get the number-one plate. But as he flew by the downed motorcycle in a blur, it appeared that Rodney was under the bike.

Jonathan let off of his throttle as he realized that Rodney wasn't broken down. He had crashed. He veered far off the course, so he could ride back to Rodney without endangering any oncoming racers.

"What a jerk," Rodney grumbled as Jonathan pulled the motorcycle off of him. "This was your chance to beat me." Rodney tried to stand up but fell over as he put pressure on his left ankle.

Jonathan took Rodney's helmet off and splashed water from his canteen on Rodney's face, then helped him get a drink.

Jonathan said, "Neither of us will be getting the number-one plate now." Just then the third-place rider roared by them on his way to victory.

"Why'd you throw away your chance?" Rodney asked. "The rescue crew will be along soon anyway."

Jonathan pulled his own helmet off and settled into the dirt next to Rodney. He looked over and smiled. "It's a God thing, Rodney," he said.

"Hey," Rodney said.

"Yeah?"

"Thanks."

Repay no one evil for evil. Have regard for good things in the sight of all men. . . . Do not be overcome by evil, but overcome evil with good.

Romans 12:17,21 NKJV

God Speaks:

Doing the right thing isn't always easy. But giving someone a break, helping them out, being a friend even when it represents a sacrifice is what grace is all about. I poured out My grace on you. I want you to do the same for others.

Someone to Talk to

I held my breath as Mrs. Dailey announced the leads for the school Christmas play, *Amahl and the Night Visitors.* "The part of Amahl will be played by Jamie Parker," Mrs. Dailey said as she smiled at the blond, curly-haired guy I'd been madly in love with ever since the beginning of the year.

My hopes soared. Now that Jamie had been given the part of Amahl, I wanted the female lead more than ever. Even though it meant playing Amahl's mother, I'd give it my best if it meant I'd be with Jamie.

In my mind I could hear Mrs. Dailey announcing my name and imagine the smile on Jamie's face as he looked across the room and saw that I was his leading lady.

My fantasy evaporated with Mrs. Dailey's next words.

"Amahl's mother will be played by Jenny Wallace," she said.

I turned with disbelief to my best friend, Jenny. She looked just as surprised as I did but a lot more excited.

"Congratulations," I finally managed. "You got the part."

I wondered if my words sounded as hollow and insincere as they felt. *How could this happen?* I wondered. *I've gotten the lead in all my school plays since elementary school. Doesn't Mrs. Dailey like me? Wasn't I good enough?*

As if in answer, Mrs. Dailey's next words came through loud and clear. "Teresa Berens, you will be one of the four shepherd girls."

A shepherd girl, I thought. *I don't want to be shepherd girl. I want the lead.*

Jenny leaned over and whispered, "Won't it be fun being in the play together?"

Fun watching you up there with Jamie while I get to be on stage for one whole minute? No way! I thought. *Maybe I'll just drop out. I'll say I have too much homework or that I plan to get a job after school.* I knew how lame those excuses would seem after I'd tried so hard for the lead.

"We'll be practicing every day," Mrs. Dailey said before dismissing us. "Plan to be here!"

At home that afternoon, I poured my heart out to Mom. "It isn't fair," I complained. "I'm sure I did a better job than Jenny. I've been in lots of plays, and she's never been in one."

"That sounds like a good reason for Mrs. Dailey to give Jenny a chance," Mom answered. "You've been in the spotlight before. Maybe it's time someone else had a turn."

"You don't understand," I said, turning to go to my room.

I realized as I walked down the hall that the only person who probably would understand my feelings was also the one person I couldn't tell—Jenny. This time the friend I usually confided in was the reason for all my misery.

I dramatically threw myself on my bed and waited for the tears to come. After all, this was how it was done on stage, wasn't it? Unfortunately, my scene was ruined when my eyes remained dry. I sighed. Mom didn't understand, and I couldn't talk to my best friend. Who else could I go to?

I rolled over and stared at the white canopy over my head. *God, are You there?* I asked silently. Then I smiled. Of course He is, I reminded myself. God is everywhere.

I stopped my silent conversation because I wasn't sure what to say. Was it okay to tell God I was angry that Jenny got the lead in the play and I didn't? Would He care that I thought Jamie was the cutest guy on earth, but he didn't even know I existed? I wasn't sure, so I rolled off my bed and headed for the phone. There had to be someone I could talk to.

When I called my friends, they were all so excited about Jenny's good fortune that I knew showing my true feelings would sound like sour grapes. Instead I decided to be the consummate actress and hide how I felt. It took everything I had.

Every day after school I sat through play practice and watched Jenny and Jamie up on stage. They worked perfectly together, and I saw why Mrs. Dailey had chosen my best friend for the part.

I knew my one line backward and forward and had already mastered the steps to the dance the shepherd girls performed, so there wasn't much else for me to do but help some of the others. It was harder than I thought to go from center stage to the supporting cast, but I played my part well. No one—not my mom, not even my best friend—knew the emotions I had bottled up inside.

Finally, one day just before opening night, I exploded. I'd had one afternoon too many of watching Jenny's stellar performance, of seeing Jamie smile at her instead of me, and of hearing Mrs. Dailey tell me to deliver my line (my one line!) with more emotion. When I got home, I was glad to find I had the house to myself. I threw my book bag on my bedroom floor and screamed as loud as I could.

"God, it's not fair," I yelled. It's just not fair!" I stood there a minute, expecting, I think, a divine lightning bolt to sizzle me on the spot for yelling at God. Nothing happened.

"I don't have anyone to talk to, God," I began. "Usually there's Mom and Jenny, but this time—" I paused and remembered how alone I'd felt over the last few weeks without my mom or my best friend to turn to. Then my words of just a couple of weeks before came back to me: *God is everywhere.*

I may have felt alone, but I had never been alone.

"You're always available, aren't You, Father?" I asked. I sat on my bed and hugged my pillow. I took a deep breath as I thought back over the weeks of painful feelings. I felt better just knowing I had someone to talk to. "Well, it's been like this, Father," I began.

I will hear, for I am compassionate.

Exodus 22:27

God Speaks:

I love you, and I genuinely care about what is on your heart and mind each day.

FYI—My last name isn't "Dang-it."
—GOD

Sophie's Choice

MRS. CHESTERFIELD: Sophie, I really hope you'll accept this role because, frankly, there isn't anyone else in the department who could come close to portraying "KATHIE" the way you can.

SOPHIE: I don't know, Mrs. C. I have so many commitments.

MRS. C.: But the success of the show depends on you.

That wasn't exactly the way it happened. Actually I went through the auditions like everyone else, chewing my nails up to the armpit the entire time. When the casting was posted, I waited until the crowd around the callboard splintered off, and then I crept up to it as if the list would lash out and cut me to ribbons if my name weren't on it.

But it was—at the top of the list, next to "KATHIE," the female lead, the character who made the audience cry into their programs, who took her last curtain call with the crowd screaming for more. It was the kind of role I'd dreamed about since I did my first backyard Cinderella at age five. Every girl in the department wanted it.

"All right, Sophie!"

I turned around to a face-freckled Eric Brolin, the Drama Club president.

"You got a plum your first time out," he said.

I shrugged and felt my face turning the color of watermelon. Why was it I could get up on stage and perform for a theatre full of people, but I could barely carry on a conversation with one other human being? "I don't know if I'll be able to pull this off," I said.

"Come on, your audition was awesome. You blew Tabby and all those other 'vets' off the stage."

"But I haven't even read the whole script yet."

Eric's grin folded his freckles into dashes as he reached into his jacket and pulled out a little white book.

I took the script from him as if it were a sacred relic. This meant more than just my first big part. I finally belonged somewhere in high school. Trying to actually live what I believed as a Christian made it hard to fit in sometimes. I brushed my fingers across the cover. Maybe now I'd found a "home."

"Will you stop massaging it and go read it?" Eric said.

There was a swish of jeans behind us, and we turned to look. People always looked when Tabatha Peters entered the area. She didn't appear to see us as she sailed past, tossing her hair back as if it, like just about everything else in the world, annoyed her to no end.

"Uh-oh," Eric said out of a hole he formed at the side of his mouth.

"What?" I said out of a similar hole.

Tabatha pivoted around, eyes wild. "Who's Sophie Crawford?"

Eric smiled woodenly and pointed to me.

Tabatha gaped for a second, then whipped around to scrutinize the callboard again—as if maybe the names had rearranged themselves.

"See you at the cast meeting after school," Eric said out of the hole. "But you'd better leave now."

I did. As I turned the corner, I heard Tabatha say, "Has she ever even done theatre before?"

MRS. CHESTERFIELD: How did you like the script, Sophie?

SOPHIE: It's a magnificent piece of writing, Mrs. C. I think I have some of the best dialogue in the play.

But that wasn't what happened either. Actually I raced through my geometry theorems first hour, so I could read the script. Before the bottom of the first page, I could see KATHIE—me—staring, angry and frightened, at her fellow girls'-home inmates, crying as she struggled to find answers, swearing at the—

Swearing.

I slapped the script onto my desk.

I hadn't been expecting iambic pentameter. KATHIE was a juvenile delinquent, after all. But I hadn't expected her to swear like that.

I hadn't expected Sophie to have to either.

SOPHIE: Eric, have you read this whole script?

ERIC: Yeah, for the first time today. Can you believe the language in this thing? We're all upset about it. A bunch of us are going to protest to Mrs. Chesterfield.

SOPHIE: May I join you?

I don't even have to mention that that wasn't what happened that afternoon at the cast meeting when I told Eric my dilemma.

"I can't do it," I said.

"Then be prepared to give your role to Tabby," he said. "She's salivating for it already."

Tabby was sitting on the edge of the stage, glaring at me. When our eyes met, hers narrowed into little points.

"Why does she hate me?" I said.

"Because you got what she wanted," Eric said. "She and about six other girls." He gave a hard little laugh. "If I were you, I'd become less of a religious fanatic for about six weeks."

I stared at my shoelaces most of the time Mrs. Chesterfield talked about rehearsals and stuff. But when she announced that the next day we'd do our first read-through, my head snapped up.

"Out loud?" I asked.

There was a smattering of snickers.

"That was the idea," Mrs. Chesterfield said. "Unless you were planning to pantomime your role."

My face was burning by then, and I just clutched the script and shook my head.

Somebody, probably Tabatha, hissed through her teeth.

"All right," Mrs. Chesterfield said, "then I'll see you tomorrow."

"I know that Sophie person has never done theatre before," I heard Tabatha say.

SOPHIE: And so, God, that's my dilemma. What's the right answer?

Suddenly in SOPHIE's room, a heavenly light seems to shimmer from the walls. At first she is frightened, until a soft voice speaks from nowhere—

Right. I tossed and turned and prayed most of the night, and there was no heavenly light and no voice, soft or otherwise. I didn't even get a peace the way I usually do after I've prayed about something and the right decision takes shape. I was still just as confused after school the next day as I had been the night before.

One minute I'd imagine myself nobly giving up the role—and crying for the next six weeks. Then I'd see myself going ahead with the role—and feeling like my mouth was full of dirt. Or worse—getting used to saying stuff like that.

"It's Sophie, isn't it?"

I looked up from my locker to meet Tabatha's smooth blue eyes. She put out her hand.

"With all the stress of the auditions and everything, I never did have a chance to welcome you to Drama Club. You'll add a lot—you're good."

Feebly I shook her hand.

"Going to rehearsal?" she asked.

I nodded stupidly.

"I'll walk with you," she said.

We took off toward the theatre together, under the stares of people who were obviously flabbergasted to see her with me, of all people.

"I hear you're having some problems with the language in the script," she said.

"News travels fast," I said.

"It's a small department. I just wanted to tell you that I admire you for having such strong convictions. I know it'll be hard to give up the role—but, there's got to be some real satisfaction in standing up for your principles like that."

At that point, my line should've gone:

SOPHIE: Oh, come on! I'm a Christian—not a moron.

Instead I just mumbled, "Thanks" and hightailed it for the other side of the theatre.

No way, I said to myself. *No way you're getting my part, sweetheart—I don't care what I have to do.*

And then I slumped down into a seat. Being jealous, wanting revenge—those were things I tried to avoid as much as swearing.

I was pretty close to tears when Mrs. Chesterfield clapped for us all to gather—and I was no closer to a decision. How was I going to do a read-through?

Slowly I made my way to the front. "Mrs. Chesterfield?" I said.

She looked up from the knot of people clamoring around her, and suddenly it was just her and me. All the time I'd dreamed up dialogues between us, I'd never written in that she would walk away from four other students and say to me, "Do you need to talk, Sophie?"

But she did. While Tabatha hissed through her teeth and Eric said out of the hole, "She's a theatre baby. Give her a break," Mrs. Chesterfield ushered me into a seat in the back row and smiled at me out of a wreath of graying curls.

"I thought you might want to talk," she said. "Eric tells me you're struggling with KATHIE's language. Come to any decisions yet?"

It looked like the only decision I'd come to was to cry. Tears were streaming down my face.

"I want this role more than anything," I said, "but I can't hear myself saying some of those words. They aren't right!"

"No, they aren't," Mrs. Chesterfield said. "I've struggled with this issue for hours myself. I don't swear, either, and I don't allow my students to in the theater. But at the same time, can you imagine a kid with KATHIE's upbringing, sitting in a detention center because she's beaten someone up to get money for drugs, saying, "Oh shucks, what am I going to do now?""

I gave a wobbly laugh.

"We'd be hooted off the stage and never make our point," Mrs. Chesterfield sighed. "And yet I don't want to offend anyone in the audience, or worse, put a student actor in a compromising position."

I could taste the tears dripping into my hanging-open mouth.

"My plan was to make changes," she went on. "I thought I was going to have to do that by myself. But maybe you and I together can replace the swearing with art. I think with your ability, you can give the role power in nonverbal ways." She smiled. "That's why I cast you."

I smeared off my face with both hands and mumbled a thank you.

She looked at me sadly. "I don't know if you should thank me or not," she said. "Out in the real world, you'd have had to make a choice. If you stay in theatre, someday you will."

"Then I'll tell them what you just said. I can give it power without the language. If I can't, I don't do the role."

"That's easy to say now," she said.

Without really meaning to, I looked down at Tabatha who had her head buried in the script. She was probably studying KATHIE's lines already.

"I know," I said.

SOPHIE: God—I have peace now. It's going to be OK. But why didn't You tell me that was the right choice?

GOD: That wasn't one of the options you gave Me, Sophie.

SOPHIE: I didn't know it was an option!

GOD: I know. That's why I told Mrs. Chesterfield.

SOPHIE's room is suddenly still. A calm settles over her, and she nestles her head into the pillow to dream—of costumes and convictions and applause.

And you want to know something?

That's exactly how it happened.

"The things that come out of the mouth come from the heart, and these make a man 'unclean.'"

Matthew 15:18

God Speaks:

If you are listening, I have a solution for even the most confusing and difficult dilemmas.

Speechless

C *= confession.*

God? It's me, Ty. I've really been messing up lately. I snapped at Mom when she tried to haul me out of bed this morning. It's tough to honor your mother when your head feels like a bowl of Cream of Wheat—Cream of Wheat. Sounds good. A bowl of Cheerios sounds better. I wonder if Mom bought any bananas.

"Oh, man!"

I rolled off my bed and sprawled on the floor. I was doing it again. I'd start out really praying hard, really getting into it, and suddenly start thinking about pepperoni or a package of double-stuffed Oreos.

"But, man—I am starving," I said out loud.

"Lucky I came along then."

I met a Sea Turtle doggie bag nose to nose. I sniffed.

"Catfish?"

"Grilled with lemon and caper sauce."

"That stuff's gross," I said, grabbing the bag.

"I'd hate to see what you'd do with something you could actually gag down." Cody shoved a pile of dirty clothes off my bed and stretched out. "How can you eat like that and never gain a pound? Never mind. I remember fifteen. You can eat everything that isn't nailed down and still look like a curtain rod."

Cody was no Jabba the Hutt now, but being my uncle, he'd always secure his seniority—just in case I forgot he was eight years older than I am.

"So what's your problem?" he asked.

"Nothing."

"Oh. Then you always lie on your back and bang your fists on the floor."

"You wouldn't believe it anyway." I tossed the empty doggie bag in the general direction of my wastebasket. "How was work?"

Cody pulled a wad of bills out of his pocket and tossed it on the bed. "A couple from Delaware on their honeymoon, somebody's uncle from Lauderdale flashing his credit cards, and two little old ladies who thought I had cute dimples and loved the scampi."

"Sounds like a pretty good night," I said. "At least you get tips. Bus boys get zippo."

"Get some dimples," he said. "Besides, Ty, that isn't the point. The money's OK, and I'm helping out your dad, but you know I'm doing this to get material for my book."

"How's that going?"

"Little old scampi-loving ladies don't make the 'Great American Novel.' I've got writer's block big time."

"Tough break," I said.

"Yeah. Hey, you got room for a pizza?"

"I've always got room for pizza," I said as we headed out the door together.

A = adoration.

Lord—I do love You. I just look around me and check out the good things in my life that You're responsible for—my dad doing well with his restaurant and for people like Kristen being on earth. Kristen—

"Aw, forget it," I said, rolling off the bed and checking myself out in the mirror. *No way Kristen is going to fall for a "curtain rod."* She probably goes for muscles. I flexed one of my biceps.

"Dream on, pal," Cody said from the doorway.

"Yeah? Who are you, Arnold Schwartzeneggar?"

Cody threw a soft punch at my middle, which I countered with a mock slap at his face.

"Remember how we used to wrestle?" he said. But he didn't wait for an answer.

He went to my window and opened the blinds. Moonlight slanted across his face in pale stripes. The dimples were grim.

"Nothing like Florida at night," he said. "I love that ocean."

"Then why do you look like you want to throw yourself to the bottom of it?"

Cody shoved his hands into his pockets and stared out.

"Still got that block thing?" I asked.

"Like the Great Wall of China. I've got all these people in this apartment building being terrorized by this unknown intruder— and I don't even know who he is myself."

"You're the author. Make him anybody you want," I said.

"Thanks, Ty," he said. "I'm really glad we had this little chat." He grinned. "So what were you doing, waiting for the muscle fairy to come?"

"No," I said, "I was praying."

"You do a lot of that," he said.

P = petition.

Please. Please, God—

That's how I always started.

I woke up depressed—and late. I'd promised my dad I'd go to the restaurant early and help, and the way the sun was squeezing through my blinds, I knew it was no longer early. And I'd fallen asleep praying.

Man, what is wrong with me? I'd been brought up to talk to God like He was a real friend. Praying had become a part of my routine—like eating.

Why was it every time I tried to pray, I ended up heading for the refrigerator or dreaming about a girl who didn't know me from the kid who bagged groceries? I must have prayer's block. I ducked for the shower.

I = intercession.

OK, God, intercession is praying for other people's needs. Please help Cody figure out how to finish his book.

Where had Cody been, anyway? He hadn't stopped by my room for a couple of days, and, come to think of it, I hadn't heard his computer going either. The whole reason he'd come to live with us at the beach was to work on his book. He worked for my dad at the Sea Turtle at night for tips and room and board, and he worked on his book during the day.

So why wasn't he writing?

I wrenched off the faucets. And why wasn't I praying?

All right, God, I'm going to get down to business.

T = thanksgiving.

Thanks, God—

"For what," I muttered, "giving me the skinniest legs on the planet?"

O = offering.

I stared down at the pan of dirty coffee cups in the sink at the Sea Turtle. What did I have to offer God? I couldn't even talk to Him.

"Yo—could we get some clean glasses out here?"

Cody—I hadn't seen him in two days.

"Keep your dinner jacket on." I handed him a flat of tumblers. "We aren't open for dinner yet. What are you doing here so early, anyway?"

"I couldn't take another blank sheet of paper. Help me set up the rest of these tables."

I followed him into the dining room.

"How come every time I walk in on you," he said, "you're muttering like a little old man?"

"It's nothing," I told him.

His dimples deepened. "And how come every time I ask you what's on your mind, you say, 'nothing'?"

"Because that's exactly what my mind is stuck on lately." I glanced at him sideways. "Do you pray?" I asked.

He snorted. "Yeah, I pray. If I didn't, I'd be out there collecting driftwood and unemployment." He steered me to another table. "Do you?"

"Yeah. No." I took a breath and continued. "I try to pray. But it seems like as soon as I say, 'Hey, Lord, it's Ty here,' I'm either thinking about food or girls, or I'm falling asleep."

"What's your approach?" he asked.

I picked up a napkin and slipped the pen out of his pocket. "It's this thing we learned in youth group." I wrote CAPITOL on the napkin. "Each letter starts a word that's a kind of prayer. Confession. Adoration. Petition. Intercession. Thanksgiving. Offering. I forget what L is for, but it doesn't much matter." I looked at Cody helplessly. "It's like I don't have anything to say to God anymore. I think I got prayer's block."

"Ah! Block! I'm an expert on that."

"What do I do about it?"

"I haven't got the slightest idea."

"Great." I picked up the flat and went for the kitchen. Cody followed, studying the napkin.

"They're still using this CAPITOL thing, huh?"

"Lot of good it does me. I can't even remember it all."

"Listen."

"What?" I picked up another flat of glasses, but Cody put his hand on my arm.

"Put that down a second, Curtain Rod," he said. "Let me be good for something. Look."

He spread the napkin out on the counter and tapped the L. "The L is for Listening."

L = listening.

"To what?"

"To God, bonehead. Don't you ever shut up when you pray?" He grinned. "Come to think of it, don't you ever shut up, period?"

I shot him a look.

"Seriously," he said. "Maybe you don't have anything to say right now. I mean, maybe your life's on a plateau. But it's a pretty sure thing that He's got something to say to you, and you're just not listening."

I hated to admit it, but it actually made sense. The worst problems I had were passing my driver's test and getting Kristen to notice me. Truth is, I'd survive if neither one ever happened.

"Whoa," I said. "Thanks."

"Great. Now, in return, go write the rest of my book for me."

I looked down at the sand bathed in moonlight except for the vague shadow of the Sea Turtle. Waves crashed. The last of the dessert forks clinked on plates. I looked up at the soft, warm Florida night.

OK, God. I'm here to say nothing.

There was quiet. It was peaceful.

I will listen to what God the LORD will say; he promises peace to his people, his saints.

Psalm 85:8

God Speaks:

You have My undivided attention every day of your life. Will you give Me yours?

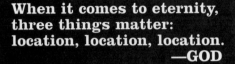

When it comes to eternity, three things matter: location, location, location.
—GOD

The Cat and the Cradle

Last winter, Margie's cat died.

"Oh, Stacy," she sniffed, "I'll never see Elmer again."

I wasn't sure what to say. Finally I said, "Maybe Elmer's in Heaven." She looked at me kind of weird, and I shrugged. "The Bible doesn't say anything about animals, but if God went to all the trouble to create them, I'm sure He must also take care of them after they die."

Margie sniffed again, but she'd quit crying.

I was going to ask Mom what she thought about it—if there is a Heaven for cats—but when she got home, she looked pretty washed out. Dad was right behind her. He closed the door carefully, then cleared his throat.

"We—um—that is—"

Mom sighed. "What your father is trying to say is, I'm pregnant."

A still coldness settled over me.

Dad nodded. "It's a surprise for us too."

"When is it due?" I asked, wishing I sounded more cheerful. It's just that I was in shock. How was I supposed to feel about becoming a big sister at the ripe old age of sixteen?

Mom's voice was tired. "The baby's due the first week of September."

"Oh," I murmured. "What are you going to do about your job?"

"I don't know," she snapped. "And I don't know where the baby's going to sleep, either."

I swallowed. That was an interesting question in that we lived in a two-bedroom condo.

Dad covered her hand with his. "Now, Tess, we'll have plenty of room. After all, Stacy is practically ready for college."

College? I wasn't even halfway through my junior year, and they were already giving away my room. Now I *knew* I didn't want to be a big sister.

Part of me wanted to pretend nothing had happened, but it was hard to ignore the discussions—and Mom's emergency dashes to the bathroom to throw up. So a couple of days later at school when Margie said I seemed a little stressed, I blurted out my news.

"Your mom's pregnant?" Margie gasped. "As in having a baby?"

"Is there another kind?" I snapped. "Margie, what am I going to do? I don't want to be a big sister."

Margie's mouth sagged open. "Wow. I can't imagine my mother having another baby." Just then the warning bell rang. "We'll talk more later," she said. "I've got to run. One more tardy and I've got a detention. See you at lunch."

After the shock began to wear off, I slowly started accepting, even looking forward to, the prospect of having a baby in the house. After all, I would finally have a sibling—a cute, adorable, too-little-to-be-a-pain sibling.

But it wasn't so easy for Mom to get used to the idea—probably because she kept throwing up. By the time she started to show, however, we were all getting excited. There were still a few tense moments, like the night Mom and Dad tried to figure out how we were going to pay the bills with me in college and Mom not working for a while.

But mostly there were good times, like finding a super cuddly stuffed lamb on sale at Walkers or rearranging the living-room furniture to make a corner for the nursery.

One night, I woke up and heard voices. Mom and Dad were talking softly in the living room. Getting out of bed, I poked my head through the doorway.

"What's up?" I asked. "Besides you two, I mean." My sleepy grin faded as Mom gasped and doubled over.

"Your mother's in labor," Dad said quietly, wrapping his arm around her.

"In labor?" I swallowed hard. She couldn't be. September was more than three months away.

Did babies born this early make it? I didn't know, and I shivered. Suddenly the night seemed cold.

Dad was leading Mom toward the door. "We just called the hospital. The doctor's meeting us there."

"I'm coming too," I insisted, not waiting to hear Dad's objections.

At the hospital they whisked Mom into emergency. Dad went with her while I slumped into a chair in the waiting room. It seemed like forever before Dad came through the double doors in a white gown, his face streaked with tears. I ran over to him, and he wrapped his arms around me.

"It was a boy," he whispered, his tears hot on my forehead. "But he was just too little to make it."

A boy, I thought, *I'd had a baby brother, and we'd never even had a chance to meet.* Dad and I hugged each other and cried for a while. Then he told me to go home and get some sleep. He'd stay at the hospital with Mom.

It's a good thing there's not much traffic at 4:00 A.M. because I was crying so hard that I could barely see the road. But when I stepped into the condo and saw the little nursery all ready in the living-room corner, my tears turned to anger.

Snatching up the little lamb, I flung it across the room. "Why, God?" I shouted. "How could You be so mean? First You gave us a baby we didn't want; then You made us want it; then—You took it away!"

I must have fallen asleep because it was morning when the doorbell woke me up. I stumbled across the room and pulled open the door. It was Dad. I'd forgotten that I had his keys.

"How's Mom?" I mumbled.

Dad collapsed onto the sofa. "OK. She'll be fine. She's sleeping now. I thought I'd come home, take a shower, get some clean clothes." He sounded vague, not like someone who was used to making decisions every day.

"Are you OK?" I said, realizing I'd asked about Mom but not him.

He made a little sound in his throat. "We decided last week. Emily if it was a girl; Brandon if it was a boy."

"Brandon," I echoed softly. "I would have had a brother named Brandon."

"A son," Dad agreed, "though I would have been just as happy with a daughter."

"Me too," I whispered and cuddled up against him like I hadn't in years. He wrapped his arms around me, and we sat. Just sat. I didn't even cry. I'd run out of tears.

Although I looked pretty awful, my eyelids puffy and my nose three shades pinker than my cheeks, I didn't want to stay home alone with all that time to think. So I went to school. Margie was waiting beside my locker when I arrived.

"Where were—? Wow, you look rotten." She stepped closer and peered at me.

"Mom had the baby too early," I said quickly, blinking as the hall started to blur. "We lost him."

"Is she all right?"

I nodded, then sniffed as Margie's arm came around me in a hug.

"It'll be OK," she whispered. "Really. At least you'll still have your own room when you come home from college."

My own room? I stared at her, my mouth open. How could she worry about something like that when my baby brother was dead?

The warning bell rang, and I said she'd better hurry. Mostly I just wanted her to leave. How could a friend be so insensitive? Hadn't I comforted her when her cat died?

"Maybe Elmer's in Heaven," I had said.

I remembered what I'd told her, and then I understood. She couldn't offer my any comfort because she didn't have any to give. She didn't believe in Heaven. But I did. I was still a big sister. I'd just have to wait awhile before I got to meet my baby brother. But when I did—

Finally, I smiled. When I did, we'd be together for eternity.

Now we know that if the earthly tent we live in is destroyed, we have a building from God, an eternal house in heaven, not built by human hands.

2 Corinthians 5:1

God Speaks:

Eternity is one of those things that humans just can't comprehend. But there is one thing you can understand. When it comes, do you want to spend it with Me?

Give me your worries.
I'll be up all night
anyway.
—GOD

The
Genny Gene

"Cool," Jonathon snorted, switching off the TV. Another noble American citizen makes an ethical decision that changes the face of integrity forever. And all on a Friday afternoon rerun of *Matlock.*

I ignored him because, after all, he's my seventeen-year-old brother, and I always ignore him. But I was thinking basically the same thing.

"Genevieve—telephone!" my mother shouted down from upstairs.

"It's Rachel," said the perky voice on the other end.

"I'm glad you called," I said, "I'm freaking out. I don't know how I'm going to make all these decisions that are ahead. What if I really mess up and end up being a shoplifter or something?"

"What are you talking about?"

"I'm talking about the reporter on *Matlock* who was locked up because he wouldn't reveal his source. We're maturing now, Rachel. We've got to start thinking about stuff like that."

Rachel snorted. "All I'm thinking about is that Marty wants us to go out with him tonight for pizza."

"We've got first amendment rights to worry about—and maybe even fifth—"

"Do you want to go or not?" Rachel asked.

I sighed. "Sure, what time?"

I think she said seven.

Okay, I know it sounds bizarre, but seeing that show really started some kind of mechanism going in my brain. My dad calls it the Genny Gene—this thing that starts when I get an idea in my head. All I could think about right then was: How was I going to make all the tough choices that were waiting out there?

"Hey, Jonathon!" I said. "You got any spare notebooks?"

He stuck a blue spiral out the crack of his door and watched me take the steps three at a time. "What are you doing?" he asked.

"Survey," I said.

I headed for the kitchen, where my dad had just come in from work.

"Dad," I said. "How do you make the really tough decisions—the ones that involve ethics?"

"Hi, Genny. How was your day?" he said. He gave me his here-we-go-again look.

"Dad, I'm serious. How do you—"

Dad put his hand up, which means "Genny-hush-up-and-give-me-seven-seconds-to-answer-you."

"Genny-Girl," he said, "I don't borrow trouble. Your worst problem right now ought to be what to do about that hairdo."

I clutched at my wild mop, currently tied into a ponytail on top of my head.

"Be a kid while you can," he said.

Mom suddenly yelled from upstairs, "Genny, come fold the rest of this laundry, please! Jeff, is that you? We have to be at the accountant's office in twenty minutes. Jonathon—answer the door when the man comes to fix the washer!"

If there's anyone who has to make a lot of decisions, it's her. I took to the steps again.

Mom was putting on her lipstick. She nodded toward the pile of clean laundry on the bed. Jonathon was in there, too, picking up his stack.

"Mom," I said, "when you have a really tough decision to make, how do you do it?"

"Look, sweetie," she said. "When the time comes that you do have hard decisions to make, your dad and I will be right there for you. There's more in the dryer, but don't get in the repair-man's way."

More decisions? In the dryer? I didn't get that one figured out until Mom and Dad had pulled out of the driveway and the washing machine repairman's truck had pulled in. Nobody was taking me seriously.

When I got to the laundry room, the repairman was studying the back of the washer. "I think I've found the problem, ma'am," he said.

"I'm not the ma'am," I answered. "I'm the kid. Could I ask you a question, sir?" I said.

"If it's about this brand of washer, sure."

"No, it's about making decisions. I mean, how do you do it?"

He put his hand in his back pocket and pulled out a dog-eared book. "I read the manual," he said.

"Rachel just called," Jonathon said behind me. "They're coming at 6:00. She wanted to be sure Mom and Dad were going to be gone when they got here. That's a little weird, isn't it?"

I was on the porch at 5:45, waiting for Marty and Rachel and studying the survey. So far I had three things written in the notebook.

Don't borrow trouble.

Go talk to somebody.

Read the manual.

I didn't see Marty's truck until he leaned on the horn.

"Hey, Geneveeev!" Marty yelled. He was leaning half his body out of the driver's-side window.

But my eyes were on the crowd in the bed of the red pickup. There must have been fifteen kids back there. Somebody was totally upside down, leg sticking up against the cab with a baseball cap tottering from his toes. Everybody was screaming some variation on "Gene-veeve!"

Rachel climbed out of the front seat and ran across the lawn to meet me.

"Hi," she said. "We picked up a couple more people—"

"A couple!" I said. "That's our whole youth group."

"You know them all."

"That isn't the point, Rachel," I said. "Marty's gonna have to slam on brakes or something, and somebody's going to go catapulting out of there. My luck, it'll be me."

"Marty's careful," Rachel said, voice winding up defensively.

"That'll mean a lot when we all get stopped by a cop," I said. "It's totally against the law—I read that."

Rachel looked over her shoulder at the squealing crew. "I know, Gen, but if we say we won't go—we're gonna miss out."

I looked at the crowd crammed into the back of the truck. It would be a bummer to sit at home, watching *Matlock* reruns while they went out and did delicious stuff.

It would also be a bummer to be plastered all over the road or have to make a phone call to Dad from Juvie Hall.

I grabbed Rachel's hand. "I'm not going, Rachel, and I don't think you want to, either. If we tell them together, maybe we can actually stop the whole thing."

"So you broke up the cruisin' party, huh?" Jonathon said to me a little later.

"Yeah," I said, "Rachel's gonna ask if we can all go to her house."

"So what happened to your survey?"

"Huh," I said. I couldn't believe he even remembered.

"You know, you didn't even need to take a survey," he said. "You already know how to make ethical decisions. What was that you did out there?"

"I said we shouldn't go because it was stupid to—"

"Borrow trouble?"

"Well—yeah. And because it's against the law—"

"You read the manual."

"But I had to have Rachel go with me because—"

"There's always somebody you can go to."

"Yikes," I said.

Suddenly, I looked at Jonathon for probably the first time in about five years. "Hey, Jonathon," I said slowly, "How do you make decisions?"

He licked his fingers. "Just like you did tonight. I mean, it only figures—we were taught the same way."

"Oh yeah," I said.

About a thousand questions popped into my head then, and I opened my mouth to spew at least thirteen of them at the same time. But he got the here-we-go-again look on his face and put up the hushup-for-seven-seconds hand.

"I hate to admit this," he said. "But weird as you are—I think God's doing a good job with you."

"Wow," I said. "So Jonathon," I said, "what makes you tick?"

He will never let me stumble, slip or fall. For he is always watching, never sleeping.

Psalm 121:3-4 TLB

God Speaks:

Whatever it is that you are worried, concerned, or wondering about, I have the answer.

**Have you told me lately
that you love me?**

—GOD

The Reunion

Dave Miller pushed his unruly curls back from his eyes and smiled at the next family in line for the Enchanted Voyage. "How many?" he asked for what was probably the five-hundredth time that day.

"Six."

"Take the blue boat," Dave said. He sighed. Most days he loved his job at the amusement park, but today he was anxious for his shift to be over. Between the hot sun, the long lines, and that annoying, animated caterpillar that sat at the ride's exit, telling everyone in its goofy voice to "Ha-ha-ha-have a happy day!" he thought he'd go nuts. Besides that, he had planned to meet the other two-thirds of the "Three Stooges" (as they called themselves) at break.

Dave smiled as he remembered how the Stooges had met. He and Larry had worked together earlier that summer at Kenton's Keelboat Canal. As they kept the boats moving, they talked about all kinds of things—especially their faith. They'd even started a Bible study on their breaks.

A couple weeks later, the two of them had literally bumped into Maureen ("Mo," as she preferred to be called) on the Dodg'ems, where she worked. For Dave it had been love at first sight. It had taken Mo a few days longer. Mo was also a Christian and quickly joined the Bible study. So it was that Curly, Larry, and Mo—the Three Stooges—were born. From the beginning, their Bible study had been sporadic at best. None of them meant for that to happen, but when Larry wasn't there, Dave liked to talk with Mo or walk around holding her hand. And when Mo wasn't there, Larry usually talked Dave into riding The Beast, the park's notorious roller coaster.

The caterpillar's monotonous laugh broke into Dave's thoughts. *I'd like to rip your speaker out,* he thought. As Dave turned back to his job, he saw a red-haired boy standing in front of him.

"How many?" he asked the couple behind him.

"Oh, he's not with us," a woman said. "He appeared out of nowhere."

As Dave began to survey the line of people for the boy's parents, he heard a man's voice farther back in the line. "Joshua! Where are you?"

When he realized the boy recognized the man's voice, Dave called, "Here he is!" The man came forward, looking relieved and annoyed at the same time.

"Thanks," he said, taking his son's hand, "I can't keep up with this guy."

"Why don't you two take the red boat?" Dave said, trying to keep the line moving.

Dave let his mind wander again. This job at the amusement park was an answered prayer. For weeks he'd prayed for a job that would be fun, where he'd meet new friends and maybe even find a girlfriend. The only thanks he'd given was an initial, "Way to go, God!" Dave shook his head as he realized how quickly he'd lost sight of all God had done for him. Not only had he let Bible study slide, but he never seemed to talk to God anymore either.

"Bye, Mister!" a voice said, bringing Dave back to reality. He turned to see the red-haired boy leaving the ride.

"Bye, kid," Dave said.

When his break finally arrived, Dave headed to the Dodg'ems to meet Larry and Mo. As he passed a bench, he noticed the red-haired boy sitting by himself crying. *Oh great,* Dave thought as he kept walking, *he's lost again.* A few steps later, he stopped and headed back. He couldn't just walk away.

"Did you lose your dad again, Josh?" he asked. Josh nodded and choked back a sob.

"Where'd you see him last?"

"At the Log Flume," Josh whispered.

Wonderful, Dave thought, *that's the opposite direction from where I'm heading.*

"Well, I'll take you to the Lost Parents' building. You can wait for your dad there." Dave held out his hand, but the boy remained sitting. "Come on," Dave said.

Josh shook his head. "I want you to find my dad."

"Josh, it would be better if we went to Lost Parents and—" Josh started crying again.

Dave knew he wasn't going to win. "OK. Let's go." Josh put his hand in Dave's with a confident smile. He seemed certain Dave could locate his dad without a bit of trouble.

As the two walked toward the Log Flume, Josh talked—nonstop. In between Josh's jabbering, Dave reminded him to keep an eye out for his dad. Nearing the Log Flume, Josh screamed, "Daddy!" and let go of Dave's hand. Dave saw Josh's dad up ahead talking frantically to a security officer. He turned as he heard his son's voice and opened his arms to the quickly approaching torpedo. The two met with an explosion of arms, all reaching to hug each another. Dave smiled as he watched the happy reunion.

"Josh, where were you?" his dad asked.

"I found him back where I was working," Dave said.

"Looks like you came to my rescue again," Josh's dad said. He pulled one arm out to shake Dave's hand. "Thanks for looking after Josh."

Dave watched the two walk away, still hugging as though they'd been apart for weeks, not minutes. "You're not mad, are you, Dad?" he heard Josh ask.

"No, I'm not mad. I'm just happy you're back."

Dave smiled. He headed back to the Enchanted Voyage, but instead of taking over, he jumped into a boat. "Back in a few minutes," he called to his replacement. As his boat wound through the ride, Dave blocked out the dancing marionettes and childish singing around him. He thought instead about Josh finding his dad and the joy of their reunion. Deep in his heart, Dave knew he was just like Josh—a son who had strayed. *You're not mad, are You—Father?* Dave prayed silently.

In his heart he heard God's reply. *No, I'm not mad. I'm just happy you're back.*

Father, thank You, Dave prayed, *for how You've worked in my life this summer—for my job, my friends. Thanks for being faithful, even when I haven't been.* Dave's boat slid out into the sunlight where the caterpillar waited. "Ha-ha-ha-have a happy day!"

Dave smiled. It was a happy day.

"'Love the Lord your God with all your heart and with all your soul and with all your mind.' This is the first and greatest commandment."

Matthew 22:37-38

God Speaks:

It matters to Me that you love Me, and I really want to spend time with you.

The Secret Admirer

It started with the delivery car from Roses & Ribbons, the local florist. Dustin Ribbons is in my biology class, and his dad owns Roses & Ribbons. I knew who the flowers were for—my sister, Greta. She was getting married to Kyle in three weeks, and everything in our house was wedding cake, wedding flowers, wedding dress. I was starting to see white lace in my dreams!

I peeked out my bedroom window and saw the delivery person bound up our sidewalk. If you worked at Roses & Ribbons, you had to wear a white shirt and pink bow tie. Downstairs, the doorbell rang, and I heard Greta squeal. She was in a perpetually cheerful mood. It didn't seem to bother her that in a few short weeks, she was going to be moving out.

My bedroom door opened, and Greta came in, holding an enormous bouquet of white carnations and little pink roses.

"They're beautiful." I sighed dutifully.

"They're for you, Ali."

"Me?" I grabbed the flowers. "Are you sure?"

"Oh, I'm sure," Greta said, eyeing me suspiciously. "Here's the card."

I opened the card, and my eyes skipped through the words, searching for a signature. There wasn't one. I read the words more slowly, trying to understand: *There is a friend who sticks closer than a brother.*

What did that mean? A friend?

That night at dinner, Greta was going on about another gift she had gotten in the mail.

"It's heavy," she said. "It must be a bread machine."

"I saw the Roses & Ribbons delivery car leaving," Mom said. "Did Kyle send you more flowers?"

"No." Greta looked as though she didn't like to be reminded. "Those were for Ali."

My dad's fork clattered against his plate. Mom stared at me in surprise.

"Who sent you the flowers, Princess?" Dad asked casually.

"The note wasn't signed," I told them.

"Ali has a secret admirer," Greta said smugly.

"Maybe it was a mistake," Mom said. "Someone who confused Ali with Greta."

"Maybe your Aunt Gladys," Dad teased. "She did send us a Valentine card at Christmas last year."

"So—it would have to be a mistake for someone to send me flowers?" I asked slowly.

"No, that's not what I meant," Mom said, giving Dad a "help me" look.

"Ohhhh! A secret admirer!" my friend Shannon said the next day, after I'd explained the whole thing.

"Dad thinks it was Aunt Gladys and that the flowers were meant for Greta," I said glumly.

"What's that on your locker?" Shannon frowned.

Something bright and colorful was stuck to the front of my locker. When we got closer, I saw it was a heart made from tissue paper. It was huge and gaudy.

"Did your notebook explode?"

I turned around, and there was Dustin Ribbons.

"No." I looked at Shannon, and we rolled our eyes in unison. "It's a gift from my secret admirer."

"Some gift," Dustin snorted. "They only cost two dollars."

I looked at him blankly.

"We sell those things at the store," he explained.

"Look at this!" I whispered. "There's a note."

"That's the same message I got last time. 'There is a friend who sticks closer than a brother.'"

That afternoon when I got home, Kyle and Greta were there.

"Mom, you'll never guess what I found!"

"Just a minute, honey," Mom murmured. "Are you sure the florist is going to deliver the flowers to the church by 9:00 A.M., Greta?"

The florist. Suddenly, it hit me. Maybe Dustin could help me find out who had sent me flowers. The thought of going to Dustin Ribbons for help made me wince, but I couldn't solve the mystery alone.

"We'll have the corsages ready for the grandparents," Kyle was saying.

"That's good." Mom smiled at him. He had already won her over. Sure, he was nice looking and had a great personality, but he was also taking my only sister away. I backed quietly out of the room. In less than a month, this whole wedding thing would be over, and I would be glad—but Greta would be gone.

"Ali?" Greta poked her head into my room after supper that night. "I cleaned out my room and found some stuff you might like. I thought you might like to have Murphy," she said, tossing the giant stuffed bear onto my bed.

"You're leaving everything behind," I muttered.

"I'm taking my dresser," she reminded me.

You're leaving Mom, Dad, and me behind, I thought. But I didn't want to spoil anything for her. "Sure," I said, forcing a smile. "Murphy can move into my room."

The next day at school, I managed to sidle over to Dustin Ribbons during lab.

"Is there a way I can find out who sent me some flowers?" I asked quickly.

"I guess." He looked bored. "Flowers, too, huh?"

"Those came first."

"No signature?"

"If there had been, it wouldn't be a secret admirer, now would it?" I said, trying to be patient. "But there was a message. *There is a friend who sticks closer than a brother,*" I recited.

"What does that mean?" Dustin frowned.

"It's a verse from Proverbs. I looked it up. Proverbs 18:24."

"And when were the flowers delivered?"

"Wednesday."

"I'll check into it," Dustin said as the bell rang.

"Maybe by tomorrow you'll know who your secret admirer is," Shannon said as we walked out of the building that afternoon. "Look!" Tied on the handlebars of my mountain bike was a huge pink balloon.

I rode home, the balloon bouncing along behind me. I couldn't wait to show Mom and Dad and Greta—and Kyle. His car was in the driveway, and I was disappointed. I mean, he was going to have her forever! Couldn't he leave us alone until the wedding?

Carefully, I untied the balloon and brought it inside.

"Where is everyone?"

"Upstairs," Greta called back.

I bounced up to her room. "What are you—"

Almost everything was gone. Mom was on her knees, packing some stuff, and Kyle was pulling nails out of the wall.

"Where did that come from?" Greta asked brightly.

"What are you doing?" I ignored her question, feeling a strange tightness in my throat.

"Packing. I'm not going to need much with the wedding in two weeks," Greta said. "We're taking most of the stuff over today, and I'll get the rest after the honeymoon."

I hadn't even realized that the balloon had floated out of my hand until I heard it bump against the ceiling. I was about to tell her it was from my secret admirer, but Greta interrupted me.

"Ali, I wanted to remind you—"

"What?" I asked sharply. "Not to trip over the hem of my dress, not to slouch at the reception, not to eat with my fingers?"

"Ali!" Mom's shocked voice broke into my tirade.

I ducked my head and ran out of the room. Where had all that come from? God, why am I so angry? There was a soft knock on the door. I figured it was Greta or Mom.

"Allison?"

Kyle!

"Can I come in?" he asked quietly.

"I suppose."

"Murphy," Kyle said, patting the bear. "Greta told me about him."

"She did?"

"Uh huh. She told me about your joke—that he was the brother you two never had."

"That was supposed to be a secret," I said tightly.

"I know," Kyle said softly. "But it got me thinking. You can have Murphy, Ali, but I'd like to be your brother, too. And not just your brother. Your friend."

Brother. Friend. I lifted my head and looked at him. And then I knew.

"You sent me the flowers," I whispered. "And put the heart on my locker, and the—"

"Balloon on your bike," he finished. "Guilty as charged. I just wanted you to know that you're special, Ali. All this wedding stuff—it kind of takes over, doesn't it? But if you take away all the flowers and the hoopla, what you have is still a family. A family that's getting bigger not smaller."

He understood. I could see it in his eyes. He went to a lot of trouble to prove it, too. I realized that Greta didn't even know what he had done for me.

"Can you play basketball?" I asked suddenly.

"I'm pretty good," Kyle grinned.

"Greta can't play," I told him. "It'll be nice to have someone who can actually hit the backboard."

"Let's go," he said, and I followed him down the stairs.

"Surely I am with you always."

Matthew 28:20

God Speaks:

I am the friend you wish you had—the One who always understands and never lets you down.

Who Gets the Ring?

s she followed her parents into the church dining room for the meal after her grandmother's funeral, Heather felt the weight of the diamond ring on her finger. It felt strange and out of place there.

"You're the oldest granddaughter, Heather," her grandfather had said less than an hour before, right after everyone had walked away from the graveside. "Your Grandma wanted you to have her ring. It's not a big stone, but she wore it for forty-three years. It was her engagement ring, and she never wanted to have another ring. There's no sense waiting to give it to you. It should be worn and enjoyed. I know you'll take good care of it. I'm giving each grandchild something of your grandma's today. Your cousin Beth will get the pearls."

"I miss Grandma already! I know she was sick and could never be better and that now she's in Heaven with God, but I still miss her! I can't believe I won't be able to talk to her again!"

Now Heather moved her hand so that the dining-room lights caught the facets of the diamond solitaire, sending out flashes of colored light as she slowly turned it. The gold band was worn smooth but still gleamed.

"Flashing the ring already? Isn't that a little gauche with Grandma just buried?"

Heather turned. Beth was standing beside her, looking at the ring. Beth was only six months younger than Heather, and they had always been in the same grade at school. That had helped bring on a rivalry between them. Sometimes Heather had been first, sometimes Beth, but they had never been really close friends.

"Grandpa gave it to me," Heather said. "He gave something of Grandma's to every grandchild today. He said he had planned it that way. And I see you're wearing the pearls." She nodded at the white strand that stood out against Beth's dark sweater.

"They're fake," Beth said in a low voice. "That ring's real! It was Grandma's engagement ring! It was old and very special to her. She wore it every day. These pearls were just something she wore now and then during the last few years."

"Grandpa said it was because I'm the oldest—"

"By six months! And I'm the one who was named for Grandma! I should have gotten her ring, and you should have gotten the pearls! For being born six months sooner, you get her ring! It's not fair! It was the thing she loved most too!"

"But—" Heather started, then stopped. The family was moving toward the serving table, and the pastor had stood up to pray.

A few minutes later, as her family started through the buffet line, Heather was relieved to see that Beth and her parents would be sitting at another table. She would not have to watch Beth looking at the ring and wanting it for herself.

She really thinks she should have it, Heather thought. *I never knew she felt that way! But, God, Grandpa gave it to me!* Grandma never said anything about who'd get her things; none of us even thought about it. We had only listened to the stories about how

Grandpa picked out the ring and then lost it on the way to Grandma's house to propose! And how they found it together!

She touched the ring again. It was beginning to feel at home on her finger, as though it had always been there.

Heather tried to concentrate on eating, but relatives kept coming over to talk. Many asked to see the ring, but no one seemed upset that she had been the one to get it.

I wish Beth understood too, Heather thought. It's a beautiful ring, and it meant so much to Grandma. She wouldn't like us to fight about it.

When she had finished eating, Heather stacked her dirty dishes and carried them to the table in front of the kitchen area. As she turned away, she cringed. Beth was coming with her dishes too.

"I just hope you appreciate the ring!" Beth was at her elbow. "It's a real family heirloom!"

"Oh, I do appreciate it! Beth, Grandpa gave it to me. I couldn't say no even if I had wanted to. And I can't give it back either! He said Grandma wanted me to have it because I'm the oldest granddaughter."

Suddenly, to Heather's surprise, she saw tears in Beth's eyes.

"I know." Beth sighed softly. "You are the oldest. It's not your fault or mine; it's just the way it happened. And I know Grandma wanted her oldest granddaughter to have it. But I loved that ring and all the stories Grandma told about it. Sometimes she even let me try it on. When I was little, it would come right off if I didn't hold my hand up in the air." She straightened her shoulders. "So now it's yours, the way Grandma wanted. I know you'll take good care of it."

Beth whirled around and hurried back to where her parents were still talking with other relatives.

"The ring looks nice on you, Heather."

"Grandpa! I didn't see you come up. I—I love the ring. I just wish—"

"That there was one for Beth too?" her grandfather asked.

Heather stared. "How did you know?"

"Your grandmother wanted to see that all her favorite things went to the right people. She wasn't sure about the ring. There's so little difference between your age and Beth's. But she wanted her oldest granddaughter to have it, and she said that was you. She was afraid Beth would feel badly about it. I've been watching you and Beth, and I can tell she's disappointed. I hope she'll understand one of these days and treasure the pearls as much as she would have the ring."

Heather put her arms around her grandfather and hugged him tight. She knew now how hard the decision had been for her grandmother and him to give her the ring.

"I understand, Grandpa," she said. "And I know Beth loves the pearls, too." She glanced over her grandfather's shoulder in time to catch Beth's eye. Her cousin shrugged and looked away. Heather knew that Beth had finally accepted their grandparents' decision.

"Grandpa!" Heather suddenly knew what to do. "Beth and I can share the ring! I'd only wear it to church and on very special occasions. We can take turns wearing it to church, and we can each wear it at special times! Beth would take as good care of it as I will!

Her grandfather wiped a hand across his eyes. "You'd do that, Heather? Oh, your grandmother would have liked that! It would be a wonderful way for both her oldest granddaughters to enjoy her ring! You might even share the pearls, too."

Heather smiled and took her grandfather's hand. "Come on. Let's go tell Beth!"

Command those who are rich in this present world not to be arrogant nor to put their hope in wealth, which is so uncertain, but to put their hope in God, who richly provides us with everything for our enjoyment. Command them to do good, to be rich in good deeds, and to be generous and willing to share. In this way they will lay up treasure for themselves as a firm foundation for the coming age, so that they may take hold of the life that is truly life.

1 Timothy 6:17-19

God Speaks:

Loving people more than things is always pleasing to Me.

Darwin says to tell you
that he was wrong.
—GOD

Why Giraffes Don't Sunburn Their Tongues

J odi hurried into the children's zoo and headed toward the group of students. They were already busy taking notes. She flipped open her notebook. "Keep all the children together when you bring them in—" Jodi tried to concentrate on the man's instructions, but someone was tugging on her shoe.

"Stop it," she muttered, glancing down. Not someone. Something. A shaggy gray goat—calmly eating her shoelace! "Cough it up!" Jodi ordered, balancing on her other foot as she tried to pull the lace out of its mouth.

The old goat glanced up at her, totally unimpressed. Its dirty-white goatee swayed back and forth as it chewed and chewed.

"It's my shoelace!" she muttered, pulling harder. Suddenly the lace slipped loose. She stumbled backward, sitting down hard in the dusty barnyard. The teacher stopped talking. Except for a few distant moos, the children's zoo was suddenly totally quiet. Everyone in the training class was staring at her. It happened a lot, that staring. She didn't think she'd ever get used to it.

"The goat was eating my shoelace," she explained quietly.

"That's something to warn the children about," the teacher cautioned them, edging through the group. "The goats can get pretty aggressive." Stopping in front of Jodi, he held a hand down to her. "Need some help up?"

Jodi sighed, then grabbed his hand and pushed to her feet. She cringed at the gasps and muttered surprises.

"Hey," someone called, "it's Shaquille O'Neal's sister!"

"How's the weather up there?" someone else cracked.

The same as it is down there, Shorty. But Jodi didn't say it. She'd already learned it didn't help. Instead, she felt herself slouching, trying to slump below the other heads around her.

At home she didn't have to. With two brothers over 6'5", she was the shrimp in the family. But since she'd hit six feet the winter before, outsiders didn't seem to notice anything else. And of course everyone assumed she was practically rabid about basketball.

Not everyone, she admitted, drifting to the back of the class as they followed the path from the children's zoo toward the monkey house. Mrs. Thompson, her Sunday-school teacher, was the one who had suggested she take the docent training at the zoo.

"You'd make a wonderful guide for the school children that visit," her teacher had told her. That bit of encouragement and Jodi's natural interest in animals had been all she needed. Three Saturdays hadn't seemed like much to give up for training, and she'd already signed up to lead tours in the fall.

"Our primate exhibits are undergoing extensive renovation," the zoo teacher explained, pointing out a long building surrounded by stacks of cement blocks and trucks. "We're trying to incorporate the latest scientific developments regarding evolution."

Jodi cringed, hearing the scornful echo of her mother's warning. "The next time that teacher tries to tell you about evolution, you tell him to look close at a newborn baby. Those tiny fingers and toes. A working heart and lungs. And nine months before, that baby wasn't anything but a sparkle in the daddy's eye. That's no descendant of a monkey! That's a miracle from God."

Jodi sighed. It had been a long year, trying to defend creation in her science class, but at least she wouldn't have to worry about those arguments on her zoo tours. She'd signed up for preschool and kindergarten classes. Evolution wouldn't be nearly as important as knowing where the nearest restroom was.

As the teacher led them out of the construction zone, he promised, "We'll be giving all the docents a refresher course on primates and specific information on the new exhibits before they open next spring. In the meantime, let's head toward the pond and our African animals."

Jodi kept to the back of the group, following along the black-top path. Her map showed elephants, gazelles, rhinoceroses, and giraffes. Their group stopped at the giraffes first, and as Jodi leaned on the cold, metal railing and stared at the gangly animals, she felt a kinship with them.

"The giraffe is uniquely suited to its environment," their teacher explained, his voice carrying in the early-morning quiet. "Mature males average sixteen feet tall. This height advantage ensures they'll find sufficient food in the upper branches of trees where competing animals can't reach. Currently, one of our females is pregnant. The gestation period is about fifteen months, and she's expected to give birth this fall. The zoo will have a birthday party when the little one is born." He chuckled. "Well, not too little. Giraffes are about six feet tall at birth."

"Six feet!" Someone giggled, and from the corner of her eye, Jodi saw a boy pointing toward her. She just kept staring at the giraffes across the moat, wondering if she'd feel like a freak for the rest of her life.

"Yes, six feet," the teacher assured him solemnly. "If the baby were much shorter, it would starve."

Jodi looked up at that. "Why?" she asked softly.

"It couldn't reach its mother to nurse." There were more giggles, but the teacher ignored them. "The giraffe is uniquely adapted in another way. Most animals have light-colored tongues, but the giraffe's is dark. Can anyone guess why?"

"They eat a lot of chocolate?" another girl guessed.

The teacher shook his head. "Hardly. Most animals bend their heads and eat from the ground, but the giraffe reaches up and wraps its tongue around leaves, pulling them down off the upper branches. The tongue has no shadow or shade to shield it from the sun. It's constantly exposed to the brilliant sunlight of the African plains. If it weren't dark, the giraffe's tongue would get sunburned."

"Wow," a few voices murmured.

The teacher nodded. "As I said, the giraffe is truly a unique animal. It has been well served by evolution."

"No," Jodi whispered, turning back to stare at the lanky brown animals. Not evolution. God. Why couldn't they see it? How could they give credit to some mysterious force based on the odds of survival instead of an omniscient God who realized eating from the treetops would be a good food source, if you didn't have to worry about sun burning your tongue? A God so loving He knew it would be too dangerous for a mother giraffe to nurse her baby lying down, so He made sure the baby was tall enough to eat standing up?

The same God who made you. The thought shot through Jodi's head, and she froze.

The God who made me? Who made me six feet tall and counting? Who knew people would laugh and point but made me like a skyscraper anyway?

Something tugged on Jodi's pants, and she glanced down. Not something. Someone. A little boy, who just joined the group, stared up at her with solemn eyes.

"Hey, lady," he asked, "how come you're so tall?"

"Andrew," a woman hissed, rushing up to him.

"It's OK," Jodi murmured automatically. And then, finally, it really was OK. Sinking down, she looked the little boy in the eye. "Hey, Andrew, I'll tell you why I'm so tall. But first, I've got a question for you. Why don't giraffes sunburn their tongues?"

The heavens are *Yours, the earth also* is *Yours;*

The world and all its fullness,

You have founded them.

Psalm 89:11 NKJV

God Speaks:

Take a minute to think about the wonders of the world around you—the beauty, order, and consistency. Now consider that you are the most important and most beloved of all I have made. I said it, so it must be true!

Dear One,

If this book has been a thought-provoking journey for you and you would like to learn more about Me, spend some time reading My letter to mankind—the Bible. Find a version that speaks to you in your everyday language.

Most of all, I want to develop a relationship with you. Talk to Me, and listen to what I have to say. Join a Bible-study group, and find a church where you can fellowship with other people who love Me. Ask lots of questions. Tell them you're new at this "God thing." They'll understand.

And remember . . . you are never alone. I am always with you.

Love,
GOD

We invite you to learn more about the GodSpeaks™
campaign by contacting us at our Web site:

www.GodSpeaks.org

Additional copies of this book and other
titles in the GodSpeaks™ series
are available from your local bookstore.

If you have enjoyed this book, or if it has impacted your life,
we would like to hear from you.

Please contact us at:

Honor Books
Department E
P.O. Box 55388
Tulsa, Oklahoma 74155

Or by e-mail at info@honorbooks.com